T0208443

(My Version)
The Best 17th Century
Virginia, Maryland
and Massachusetts
Black Cooks

(My Version)
The Best 17th Century
Virginia, Maryland
and Massachusetts
Black Cooks

First Thanksgiving and Christmas Emanuel Cookbook

BOOK SERIES NO. 1
Pre and Post Slavery Reviews

SHARON KAYE HUNT

To order additional copies of this book, contact:
Xlibris
1-888-795-4274
www.Xlibris.com
Orders@Xlibris.com
807605

CONTENTS

Part II Maryland

Part III Massachusetts

DEDICATION

The author is thankful for the favor of Jesus Christ in giving her ideas and she dedicates all her work to Him. Also, she dedicates the Book Series to all descendants of slaves, and the world as a whole who has profited from the slaves food knowledge and preparation methods.

"Commit thy works to the Lord and thy thoughts
will be established" Proverbs 16:3

The author is especially thankful to her parents Dewey and Repol Hunt for their wealth of teaching about slavery.

DISCLAIMER

The information about slaves' food selections and menu development were developed by the author. All recipes were developed by the author and do not represent ideas of others.

Biblical scriptures were selected by the author.

PREFACE

Each year a history of the First Thanksgiving in the United States is noted and the date of 1621, but no mention of the slaves first thanksgiving even though the some slaves arrived in Virginia in 1619.

Therefore, the author has written eight books for the Series. The purpose of the Series- Food Revelations from Heaven (Jehovah - Jireh) to Slaves is to propose what the first slaves may have prepared and eaten for their first Thanksgiving and Christmas dinners.

To gain some insights in the slaves' lives, some slave narratives that are in the public domain were consulted.

CHAPTER 1

INTRODUCTION

The name of the first book in the Series is -The Best 17th Century Virginia, Maryland and Massachusetts Black Cooks First Thanksgiving and Christmas Emanuel Cookbook. The cookbook is centered around what the slaves may have prepared for their meals and how they may have prepared the meals. The cookbook is divided into three parts. Part I -Virginia; Part II-Maryland and Part III-Massachusetts.

Each part is divided into food items, information about the state, pre- and post-slavery reviews, regions of each state, and biblical scriptures.

INFORMATION ABOUT SLAVERY – PRE AND POST

Slavery in America Before the Constitution

Beginning in 1619, the first slaves were brought to Virginia. The southern planters were dependent on slave labor to work in the fields of cotton, rice and other duties around the plantation. The slave labor was free.

When the Constitution was written, the slaveholders did not want Congress to be given the power to stop slave trade. The original Constitution was written in 1787. As a compromise, the writers of the Constitution agreed that Congress would not stop the slave trade for 20 years.

After 1808, new slaves could not be brought into the country. However, slavery continued in some states.

Slaves were bought, sold and kept in slavery until 1865.

Freedom came to most slaves after two hundred or more years in slavery. Even though the Emancipation Proclamation was issued in 1863, the end of slavery marked by the passing of the 13th Amendments to the Constitution and the end of the Civil War in 1865. Many of the slaves did not receive notification until later.

For example, the Texas slaves did not receive the news until June. Therefore, Texas African-American celebrate Juneteeth-June 19 was Emancipation Day in 1865. Georgia former slaves celebrate May 12, 1865.

Emancipation Proclamation

The Civil War started in Sumter County, South Carolina in 1861. Slavery was one of the cause why the Civil War broke out.

The Emancipation was written by President Abraham Lincoln in 1863, two years after the War began.

It stated the Emancipation Proclamation, that all slaves in the rebellion states-the confederated states-were free. It did not free the slaves in the states that were loyal to the Union. All slaves were freed after thee ending of the Civil War.

The Civil War Amendents-13th, 14th and 15th Amendments were passed to give slaves freedom.

The 13th Amendment was approved in 1865. The Amendment made slavery illegal.

The 14th Amendment was approved in 1868 to protect the right of the freed slaves. It along with Bill of Rights, protect the rights of citizens. The Amendment says any state deprive (deny) any person of life, liberty or property, without due process of law (the right to be treated fairly, nor deny to any person within

Its jurisdiction (boundaries) the equal protection of the law.

The 15th Amendment approved in 1870, guaranteed black male citizens the right to vote. Neither black nor white women had the right to vote until 1920.

BIBLICAL SCRIPTURE

Psalm 35:1

Plead my cause, O Lord, with them that strive with me: fight against them that fight against me.

PART I
VIRGINIA

CHAPTER 2

FIRST VIRGINIA SLAVES POSSIBLE AVAILABLE FOOD AND COOKING SOURCES

1.   Foods   Sources

a. Meats-beef, pork   plantations, slaveholders

opossums, squirrels, deer   wild life

Wild turkeys

Fish-freshwater and sea

     Ocean, rivers and lakes

     Smokehouses

b. Vegetables   Powhatan Indians

Carrots, beans, squash,

Corn, greens

Rutabagus, turnips, cabbage

d. Dry beans and peas   slave ship from Africa

e. Flour and meal   slave ships and Indians

f. Fruits   wild fruits

g. Peanuts   Slave ships

h. Milk and Dairy   plantation and slave holders

i. Sorghum, rice, yams Okra   slave ships

j. Eggs, honey   Slave holders

k. Salt and seasonings   slaves transport

l. Food storage   Slaves knew how to preserve fresh fruits and vegetables from summer to winter months by using pine straw and digging pits in the ground. They knew how to preserve watermelons, cantaloupes, pears and apples.

m. Curing meats and smokehouse   Africa

COOKING SOURCES

1. Cooking Utensils and Heating   Sources
   a. Large black pots   Africa
   b. Black iron skillets   Africa
   c. Gourd dippers   Indians
   d. Fire wood   Indians
   e. Flint rocks   Indians
   f. Fire Hearth or place   Plantation
   g. Clay pots   plantation
   h. Hot coals   plantation
   i. Fire pits and grills   Indians

Cooking Procedures

1. The slaves could not read or write. In cooking they used their hands for measurements the amounts of ingredients needed in preparing a recipe.
2. The author used up-to-date measurements for possible amounts of ingredients intended by the slaves hand measurements.
3. For stirring in pots, the slaves used, heavy sticks made out of wood.
4. For eating, the slaves used spoons made from gourds, wood and oyster shells.

ABOUT VIRGINIA

Virginia
VA
OLD DOMINION STATE
SLAVEHOLDING FROM 1619-1865

Capitol	Richmond
History	English Settlers found Jamestown in 1607. Virginians took over much of the government from royal Dunmore in 1775 forcing him to flee. Virginians under George Rogers Clark Freed the Ohio-Indiana-Illinois area of the British forces, Benedict Arnold burned Richmond and Petersburgh for the British in 1781. In the same year, Britain's Cornwallis was trapped at Yorktown and surrendered.

STATE DATA:			
	Motto:	Sic Semper Tyrannis	(Thus always to tyrants)
	Flower:	Dogwood	
	Bird:	Cardinal	
	Tree:	Dogwood	
	Song:	Carry Me Back to Old Virginia	
	Entered Union:	Tenth of the Original 13th colonies to ratify the Constitution	
	People:	White(English, Germans and Italians), Blacks and Hispanics	
	Geography:	Land Area: 40, 817 square miles, rank: 36, Land area 39,780	
	Location:	South Atlantic State founded by Atlantic Ocean in The east and surrounded by North Carolina, Tennessee, Kentucky, West Virginia and Maryland.	
	Climate:	Mild and equable	

	Topography:	Mountain and valley regions to the west, including Blu Ridge Mountains, rolling Piedmont plateaus, tidewater, or Coastal plains, including the eastern shore.
ECONOMY	Principal industries:	Government, trade manufacturing, tourists, Agriculture
	Principal manufactured	
	Goods:	Textiles, food processing, apparel, transportation Equipment, chemicals
	Agriculture:	Chief crops: tobacco, soybeans, peanuts, Corn
	Livestock:	Cattle, hogs/pigs, sheep. poultry
	Timber:	Pine and hardwoods
	Minerals:	Bituminous coal, stone, cement, lime, sand and Gravel and sand, zinc
	Chief ports:	Hampton Roads
	Major International	Norfolk, Dutts, Richmond, Newport News
	Tourist Attractions:	Colonial Williamsburg; Busch Garden, Wolf Trap Farm, near Falls Church, Arlington National Cemetery; Mt. Vernon; home of George Washington, American Festival Park, Yorkton, Jefferson's Monticello, Charlottesville; Robert E. Lee's birth place, Stratford hall, and grave, at Lexington Appomattox; Shenandoah National Park; Blue Ridge Parkway, Virginia Beach

FAMOUS BLACK VIRGINIANS:

William Tucker and Booker T. Washington

First African were brought to Virginia from Angola, Africa Anthony and Isabella Tucker First black couple

Nat Turner's Rebellion -Southampton County, VA 1831

REGIONS OF VIRGINIA

1. Heart of Appalachia
2. Blue Ridge Highlands
3. Central Virginia
4. Chesapeake Bay
5. Coastal Virginia-Eastern Shore
6. Coastal Virginia – Hampton Roads
7. Northern Virginia
8. Shenandoah Valley
9. Southern Virginia
10. Virginia Mountains

BIBLICAL SCRIPTURE

PSALM 91:1,2

1 He that dwelleth in the secret place of the most High shall abide in the shadow of the Almighty.

2 I will say of the Lord, He is my refuge and my fortress: my God: in him will I trust.

CHAPTER 3

Two Possible First Thanksgiving Dinner and Snack Menus May Have
Been Used by the First Slaves of Virginia

I

Watermelon Cubes
Pear Compote
Blue Crab Stew
Squirrel and Carrot Soup

Roasted Wild Turkey
Fried Deer Steak

Corn Bread Stuffing
Wild Rice Dressing

Green Beans and Potatoes
Squash Casserole

Sweet Potato Pudding
Molasses Cake

Apple Cider
Snacks
Roasted Peanuts
Hickory Nuts Cookies

II

Pickled Peaches
Fried Oysters

Peanut Soup
Okra Soup

Barbeque Pulled   Pork
Fried Shrimp

Boiled   Lima Beans
Cornbread Hoecakes
Sweet Potato Custards
Molasses Pie   Buttermilk
Coffee
Snacks
Smoke Crab Legs
Syrup Candy

PRE AND POST SLAVERY REVIEWS

FIRST SLAVERY IN VIRGINIA

Slavery started in Virginia when the first slaves arrived in 1619. They came on the ship White Lion. There on the ship were 20 Africans. The ship landed on the colony of Jamestown, Virginia.

Food sources listed on the ship were flour, meats and black-eyed peas.

VIRGINIA SLAVES INFORMANTS

FORMER SLAVES and THEIR ADDRESSES AFTER FREEDOM FROM SLAVERY

1. Fannie Berry   Page Number   1
   Petersburg, Virginia
2. Charles Crawley   7
   Petersburg, Virginia
3. Minnie Fulkes Fulkes   11
   Petersburg, Virginia
4. Georgiana GiwibGiwbs (Gibbs) 707   17
   Lindsay Avenue Portsmouth, Virginia

VIRGINIA TOURIST REGION

Heart of Appalachia

1. Bluefield
2. Grundy
3. Norton
4. Town of Tazewell
5. Big Stone Gal
6. Clintwood
7. St. Paul
8. Coeburn

Counties

1. Buchanan County
2. Dickerson County
3. Lee County
4. Russell County
5. Scott County
6. Tazewell County
7. Wise County

BIBLICAL SCRIPTURE

PSALM 92:1

It is a good thing to give thanks unto the Lord, to sing praises unto thy name, O most High.

CHAPTER 4

Two Possible First Christmas Dinner and Snack Menus May Have Been Used By the First Slaves of Virginia

I

Crab Cakes

Turtle Soup

Sugar Cured Ham
Venison   Roast

Boiled Turnip Greens

Fried Corn
Fried   Potatoes

Corn cakes
Apple Cobbler
Pumpkin Pie
Corn Shuck tea

Snacks
Apple Butter/ Buttermilk Biscuits
Dried Shrimp

II

Crayfish Stew
Smoked Ham
Fried Chicken
Rice and Gravy

Sweet Potatoes
Mustard Greens

Corn Bread
Cherry Pie
Vinegar Pie

Eggnog

Snacks
Pickled Pig Feet
Baked Sweet Potatoes

PRE AND POST SLAVERY REVIEWS

Former Virginia Slaves Views on Freedom

1. Fannie Berry -Petersburg, Virginia
   Interviewed by Susie Byrd – February 1937

Civil War:

"The Colored Regiment came by behind an' when saw the colored regiment they put up the white flag, (Yo' 'member 'fo' dis red or bloody flag, was up). Now, do you know why dey raise dat white flag? Well honey, dat white flag was taken a token dat Lee had surrendered."

2. Charles Crawley -Petersburg, Virginia
   Interviewed by Susie Byrd in February, 1937

"Marsster Allen, owned my mother an' sister too, and emigrant(emigrated) here, come to dis town of Petersburg after Lee's surrender. I mean you now de ending de Civil War. My mother, sister and I came down the road in a box car, which stopped outside de out skirts; hit didn't go though de city, yes, I know when de first railroad was built, the Norfolk and Eastern and de Atlantic Coast line dey were through Petersburg and in dem days it was called de Southern."

VIRGINIA TOURIST REGION – CENTRAL REGION

CITIES

1. Charlottesville
2. Colonial
   Heights
3. Hopewell
4. Petersburg
5. Richmond

COUNTIES

Albermarle
Amelia
Caroline
Charles
City
Chesterfield
Dinwiddie
Fluvannie
New Kent
Orange
Powhatan
Prince George

Amherst
Appomattox
Buckingham
Cumberland
Goochland
Greene County
Nelson
Hanover
Louisia
Madison
Sussex
Nottoway
Prince George
Prince Edward

Henrico

Appomattox
Blackstone
Lynchburg
Scottsville
Wintergreen
Ashland
Chester
Farmville

BIBLICAL SCRIPTURE

PSALM 105:1

O give thanks unto the Lord; call upon his name make known his deeds among his people.

CHAPTER 5

APPETIZER COURSE

Possible Recipes Used by the First Virginia Slaves for Appetizers for the First Thanksgiving and First Christmas

Thanksgiving Appetizers

Watermelon Cubes

Amounts	Ingredients
4 cups	watermelon, cubes

Directions

1. Cube watermelon into 1 -inch squares.
2. Serve in coconut shells.

Pear Compote

Amounts	Ingredients
1 pound	pears, peeled
2 cups	water
½ cup	honey

Directions

1. Peel, pare and cube pears.
2. Place in a kettle on fire place
3. Pour water over pears and cook until soft.
4. Cool and stir in honey and serve.

Pickled Peaches

Amounts	Ingredients
1 pound	wild peaches, peeled
1 quart	vinegar
2	whole cloves

Directions

1. Peel peaches, place in a bowl
   And set aside.
2. In a kettle, boil vinegar and cloves for 5 minutes.
3. Pour vinegar mixture over peaches and cover for six hours serve.

Fried Oysters

Amounts	Ingredients
1 dozen	oysters shucked
2	eggs, beaten
1 cup	buttermilk
1 teaspoon	black pepper
1 ½ cups	lard, hot

Directions

1. Shuck oysters. Set aside.
2. Mix together buttermilk and eggs.
3. Set aside.
4. Stir together flour, salt an black pepper.
5. Heat lar in black skillet.
6. Dip each oyster in buttermilk mixture and then flour.
7. Fry in lard until crispy.

CHRISTMAS APPETIZERS

Crab Cakes

Amounts	Ingredients
1 pound	crab, picked
1	egg, beaten
1 teaspoon	*salt*
¼ cup	onions, minced
2 tablespoons	flour, for binding
2 cups	lard for frying

Directions

1. Pick oysters and stir in remaining ingredients.
2. Roll meat into 1-inch balls.
3. Heat lard in black skillet.
4. Fry in lard until golden brown.

PRE AND POST SLAVERY

Virginia Former Slaves
Minnie Fulkes
Petersburgh, Virginia

Interviewed by Susie Byrd -March 6, 1937

"She belonged to Dick Belcher in Chesterfield County. Old Dick sold us again to Gelaspe Graver. How fifteen of mother's children was with her having de same master.

Serving God

"Well, sometimes you know dey would, the others of 'em, keep going 'til dey fin' whar dis meeting was gwine on. Dey would come in and start whipping an' beatin' the slaves unmerciful. All dis wuz done to kee' yo' from servin' God, an' do you know some of dem, devils wuz mean an' sinful 'nough to say.

"EF I ketch you here agin servin' God I'll beat you. You haven't time to servr God. We brought you to servr us."

Civil War

"As I wuz tellin' you his ' brother wuz kept, but dey sent father, but dey sent father has' home.

Uncle Spencer was left in Prince County. All his chillen ar' still dar. I don't know de name of Yankees who carried him off."

My father waited on soldiers and after de s'render dey carried him an' his brother as far as Washington, D.C.

I think we all use to say den, Washington City. Ain't you done heard folks talk 'bout dat city? "Tis grade big city, den when de President of des here Country stay: an' in bac' days it wuz known as 'viden' lin' for de North an' South. I done hear dem white folks tell all 'bout dem things dee line."

Yankees

"Lord, Lord Honey, dem times too often and some Yankees took lots of slaves away an' dey made homes. Am' whole heap of families lost sight of each other."

Food

Us had plenty of food such as corn bread, butter milk, sweet potatoes, biscuits.

Slaves Whipped

Slaves den dey would handcuff dem and beat 'em unmerciful, slaves 'beellied. I done seed dem whip 'em wid a strap sol with cat of nine tails."

23

Masters when they couldn't catch 'em they didn't bother sometimes de slaves would go an' take up an' live at other places; most of 'em liv ed in de woods off of taken things such as hogs, corn, an' vegetables from other fo'ks farm. Well, if dese slaves was caught, dey was sold by their new masters to go down south.

Dey told me dem Masters down South wuz so mean to slaves would let 'em work dem cotton fields 'til dey fall dead wid hoes in dare hands den would beat dem.

Slaves Auction

There was an auction block!

I saw right here in Petersburg on the corner of Sycamore Street and Bank Street. Slaves were auctioned offin de highest bidder. Some refused to be sold by dat I mean, cried, Lord, Lord: I done seen dem young 'ums faint and kick like crazy fo'kes child and ws piriful to see 'em."

Education

"I think by Negro gitten educated he has profited an' dis here younger generation to is gwine to put off dese poor white folks."

Praising God

"In dem back days child, meeting was carried on jes like usdo today, somewhat.only difference is the slave dat knowed de most'bout de Bible would tell and explain what God had told him in a vision(yo' young folks say, 'dream) and dis freedom would come to pass; an' den dey prayed for dis vision to come to pass, an' dere when de paddy rollers would whip 'em."

VIRGINIA TOURIST REGION

BLUE RIDGE HIGHLANDS

Cities

1. Abingdon
2. Bristol
3. Galax
4. Marion
5. Blacksburg
6. Christainburg
7. Damacus
8. Pulaski
9. Radford
10. Wytheville

Counties

1. Bland
2. Carroll
3. Floyd
4. Giles
5. Grayson
6. Montgomery
7. Patrick
8. Pulaski
9. Washington
10. Wise
11. Wyeth

BIBLICAL SCRIPTURES

PSALM 106: 1

Praise ye the Lord, O give thanks unto the Lord: for he is good: for his mercy endureth forever.

CHAPTER 6

SOUP AND STEWS COURSE

Possible Recipes First Virginia Slaves May Have Used for Soups and Stews

THANKSGIVING SOUPS AND STEWS

Blue Crab Stew

Amounts	Ingredients
1 pound	Blue crab meat, Picked chopped
1 medium	onion, minced
½ pound	white potatoes, cubed
½ cup	lard
2 strips	salt pork, cubed
1 quart	milk
2 tablespoons	flour
1 teaspoon	salt
½ teaspoon	black pepper

Directions

1. Pick crab meat and set aside.
2. In a large Dutch oven, fry salt pork until crispy. Remove meat and cook onions.
3. Ad cubed potatoes and cook until softened.
4. Remove excess fat and slowly add in milk.
5. Stir well and add crab meat. Cover and cook for 10 minutes.
6. Sprinkle in flour. Stir well and stir in salt and pepper.
7. Cook for 10 minutes.

Squirrel Soup

Amounts	Ingredients
1	squirrel cleaned, washed and cut up
1 gallon	water
1 tablespoon	salt
1 pound	white potatoes, cubed
2 tablespoon	lard
1 pound	carrots, cut across
½ pound	blackeyed peas, washed and picked

Directions

1. Skin, clean and wash squirrel. Cut into pieces.
2. Place in a big black pot over heat coals, Place meat and water with salt in black pot and cover.
3. Cook for one hour. Stir add remaining ingredients cover and cook until desired doneness.

Peanut Soup

Amounts	Ingredients
2 cups	peanuts, raw
2 strips	salt pork
1 quart	water
1 quart	milk
1 teaspoon	salt

Directions

1. In a large black pot add peanuts and salt pork. Cook until peanuts are done. Black pot should be heated over coals.
2. Gradually add in water and cook until peanuts are soft.
3. Mash peanuts to make a smooth paste.
4. Gradually add in milk stirring well. Cover and cook for 1 hour.

Okra Soup

Amounts	Ingredients
1 ½ quarts	water
2 strips	salt pork, cut into cubes
1 pound	okra, cut up
2 tablespoons	salt
½ cup	onion, minced
2	pepper pods, chopped
2 cups	squash, cut up
1 cup	carrots

Directions

1. Place water and salt pork into a large black pot and heat over hot coals for 30 minutes or until meat is done.
2. Stir in cut up okra, salt and onion. Cover and cook for 30 minutes.
3. Add remaining ingredients.

CHRISTMAS SOUPS

Turtle Soup

Amounts	Ingredients
1	turtle, shell and insides removed, cleaned and meat cut up
2 gallons	water
2 teaspoons	salt
¼ medium	onion, minced
2 pods	hot red pepper
2 tablespoons	flour, for thickening
1 pound	wild rice

Directions

1. Clean turtle by removing shell, feet and internal organs. Clean muscle meat and chop.
2. Wash meat and place with water and salt in a large black over hot coals. Bring to a boil and cook for 45 minutes.
3. Stir in remaining ingredients and cook for 1 hour. Add wild rice. And cook until done.

PRE AND POST SLAVERY REVIEWS

Virginia Former Slaves
Georgiana Giwbs (Gibbs)
Portsmouth, Virginia
707 Lindsay Avenue
February 15,1937
Soap

"We had a washing house. Dere uz five women who done de washing an' ironing. Dey had to make de soap. Dat was done by letting water drip over oak ashes. Dis oak ash lye, and dis wuz used in making soap.

After de clothes had soaked in de lye soap and water, dey put de clothes on tables and beat 'em 'till dey wuz white.

Slaves

500 slaves on the plantation.

Marriage

"Yer had to jump over the broom three times. Dat was de license."

Candis Goodwin, 80 years
Cape Charles, Virginia

Praise

"Sometimes de ol' folks uster to get togedder in de quarters – kitchen tuh shout and pray.

Who's yuh pappy? Who's yuh pappy? Ah jes' say "Turkey buzzard lay me an' de sun hatch me' an' Den gown 'bout my business."

Father in the Civil War

"Lemme tell yuh 'bout hihow he did in de war. He big man in de war. He drill soldiers ev'y day.

Firs' he be in one dem companies -Company "C". Den he worked up to be sergeant -major, in de Tenth Regiment."

Father

"He was taken to camp and assigned as a cook. At first he was not very successful in his job, but gradually improvement was shown. He was what wages he would accept. It was such a pleasure to know he had escaped the clutches of slavery, he did not ask for wages, but instead he was willing to work for anything they would give him, no matter how small, as long as he didn't have to return to slavery.

Within a short period he was given a uniform and guns as fully enlisted as a soldier, in the 19th regiment of Wisconsin, Company E. Here he remained in service until November 1862.

After which time he returned to Norfolk to spend time with his mother, who was still living. While sitting in the doorway, one day, with his mother, he was again confronted with the proposition of enlisting. He agreed to do so for one year.

Charles Grandy, 96 years old

Civil War

The news of war and the possibility of negroes enlisting as soldiers was truly a step closer to answering of their prayers for freedom. Upon hearing the good news, Grandy joined a few others in the break for freedom.

One night, he and a close friend packed a small quantity of food in a cloth and about midnight to join the northern army. Traveling at night most of the time, they were constantly confronted With danger.

Arriving in Norfolk

Grandy and his friend decided to take different roads of travel. Several days and nights found him wondering about on the outskirts of Norfolk, feeding on wild berries. While picking berries along a ditch bank, he was hailed by a Yankee soldier, who having come in contact with runaway slaves before, greeted him friendly, and questioned him of his home and knowledge of work."

VIRGINIA TOURIST REGION

VIRGINIA MOUTAINS

Cities

1. Bedford
2. Bachanan
3. Clifton Forge
4. Covington
5. Fincastle
6. Hot Springs
7. New Castle
8. Roanoke
9. Rocky Mount
10. Salem

11. Troutville
12. Vinton
13. Warm Springs

Counties

1. Allegheny County
2. Bath County
3. Bedford County
4. Botetourt County
5. Craig County
6. Franklin County
7. Highland County
8. Roanoke County

BIBLICAL SCRIPTURES

PSALM 110:1

The Lord said unto my Lord, sit thou at my right hand, until I make thy enemies thy footstool.

CHAPTER 7

ENTRÉE COURSES

Possible Recipes Used by the First Virginia Slaves for Entrees

THANKSGIVING ENTREES

Roasted Wild Turkey

Amounts	Ingredients
1 -15 pound	wild turkey
2 tablespoons	salt
2 gallons	water
2 tablespoons	lard

Directions

1. Clean and wash wild turkey.
2. Fill a black pot with water add the wild turkey and salt.
3. Boil the turkey in the water, until tender.
4. Drain and cool off.
5. Rub lard over cooled turkey. Place turkey over Hot coals on a home made rack for roasting meat.
6. Roast for 2 hours or until desired doneness.
7. Slice and serve.

Fried Venison Steaks

Amounts	Ingredients
8	Venison Steaks, cut into 8"" X 2" Steaks
2 quarts	milk
2 teaspoons	salt
1 ½ teaspoons	black pepper
1 pound	flour
2 cups	lard

Directions

1. Soak steaks into milk for 4 hours. Drain.
2. Wash meat. Pat dry.
3. Season with salt and black pepper
4. Dredge in flour on both sides.
5. Heat lard to hot in a skillet in the fire place.
6. Fry meat in lard to golden brown on both sides.

Barbeque Pulled Pork

Amounts	Ingredients
1	whole hog/ split into half
2 cups	lard
2 cups	salt
1 cup	black pepper
1	Barbecue pit
Pit should be built to hold two halves of pork	
2 gallon	vinegar
4 gallons	molasses
1 quart	water

Directions

1. Clean and wash hog halves. Rub each half with lard.
2. Combine black pepper and salt in a big bowl.
3. Evenly sprinkle salt and pepper over each half.
4. Cover and cook meat over low heat for 24 hours.
5. Pull pork to check for doneness.
6. For pull pork, pull all the meat off bones. Chop the meat. Prepare sauce.
7. In a large black pot, cook vinegar, molasses and water. Stir well and cook on low heat for 2 months.

Fried Shrimp

Amounts	Ingredients
2 pounds	shrimp, cleaned deveined
2	Eggs, beaten
2 cups	buttermilk
½ pound	flour
1 teaspoon	salt
1 teaspoon	black pepper
3 cups	lard

Directions

1. Clean and wash shrimp
2. Beat eggs and place in a bowl.
3. Place buttermilk in a bowl.
4. Stir flour salt and black pepper.
5. Heat lard.
6. Dip each piece of shrimp in eggs then flour and then buttermilk and flour again.
7. Fry shrimp until golden brown.

CHRISTMAS ENTREES

Sugar Cured Ham

Amounts	Ingredients
1-10 pound	sugar cured ham
3 gallons	water
2 cups	molasses

Directions

1. Place sugar cured ham and water into large black pot and boil for 1 ½ hours.
2. Remove from water and discard water. Cool down.
3. Rub ham with molasses.
4. Place in a large black skillet and cover and cook over low coals for 1 hour.
5. Cool and slice.

Venison Roast

Amounts	Ingredients
1 – 5 pound	venison roast
½ cup	lard
1 tablespoon	salt
½ teaspoon	black pepper
1 cup	water

Directions

1. Trim roast and rub with lard.
2. Sprinkle salt and pepper.
3. Place in a large black pot with cover. Add water. Cover.
4. Place over low coals and cook for 1 hour.
5. Check for doneness. Cool and slice.

Smoked Ham

Amount	Ingredients
20 pound	smoked whole ham

Directions

1. Dig out in the ground a pit 4' x 4' and fill with hot coals.
2. Place a strip of tin over coals.
3. Place ham on tin. Place a second piece of tin over ham.
4. Cook for 4 hours on low heat.
5. Check until desired doneness.

Fried Chicken

Amounts	Ingredients
1 -2 ½ pounds	fryer
1 teaspoon	salt
1 teaspoon	black pepper
21/2 cups	flour
2 cups	lard

Directions

1. Wash and cut up chicken.
2. Season with salt and pepper
3. Roll in flour.
4. Heat lard up in large black skillet in a fireplace.
5. Place large pieces in hot lard. Cook for 10 minutes on one side and 5 minutes on the second sides.
6. Drain.

PRE AND POST SLAVERY REVIEWS

VIRGINIA FORMER SLAVES

1. Charles Grandy
   Norfolk, Virginia
   Interviewed by David Haggard-February 26, 1937

   "Born: March 19, 1848 in Mississippi imprisoned in Norfolk and later taken to Hickory Ground, Virginia and then sold. Slaves were often taken to rural districts in carts, and sold to owners of plantations as they were needed."

   Slave Gardens

   "Slaves were allowed to have small quantities of whiskey, even during the day of worship, to use for medicinal purposes. It was common occurrence to see whiskey being sold at the foot of the hill near the churchyard."

2. Della Harris
   Petersburg, Virginia
   Interview taken February 5, 1937 by Susie Byrd

   Owner

   Belonged to Peter Buck Turnbull, Warenton, N.C. In North Carolina- In dem days you have to take master and mistress' name.

   Surrender: I was 13 years old at de time un Lee's surrender.

   Indian Mother

   "My mama was a genuine Indian. Some people dey you can't own IndiaNS. I don't know how come, but I do know she was owned by these people, but she surely was de INDIAN."

Lighting Days

"Talking about lightning days. Its lightning at everybody house. Lord have mercy on dese here young folks and deliber me from the plantation I pray."

VIRGINIA TOURIST REGION

COASTAL VIRGINIA -Hampton ROAD

Cities

1. Charles City
2. Chesapeake
3. Franklin
4. Hampton
5. Mathews
6. Newport News
7. Norfolk
8. Poquoson
9. Portsmouth
10. Smithfield
11. Smithfield
12. Suffolk
13. Virginia Beach
14. Virginia Beach
15. Williamsburg
16. Yorktown
17. Yorktown

Counties

18. Charles City
19. Isle of Wight
20. James City

21. New Kent
22. Southampton
23. Surry
24. York

COASTAL VIRGINIA -EASTERN SHORE

Cities

1. Accomax
2. Cape Charles
3. Chincoteague Island
4. Exmore
5. Onancock
6. Tangier Island
7. Wachapreague

Counties

1. Northampton
2. Accomack

BIBLICAL SCRIPTURES

PSALM 111:5

He hath given meat unto them that fear him; he will ever be mindful of his covenant.

CHAPTER 8

STARCH COURSES

Possible Recipes Used by the First Slaves of Virginia for Starches

THANKSGIVING STARCHES

Cornbread Dressing

Amounts	Ingredients
2	turkey wings
1 medium	onion, chopped
1 teaspoon	salt
1 gallon	water
4 cups	cornbread, crumbled
2 cups	biscuit crumbs
1 teaspoon	black pepper
1 teaspoon	salt
1 medium	onion, minced
½ teaspoon	sage
3	eggs, boiled

Directions

1. In a large black pot, boil turkey wings in water with onion and salt until done.
2. Remove turkey wings from water, chop finely and save broth.
3. Set aside.
4. In a large pot, stir together turkey broth with crumbled corn bread and other ingredients.
5. Stir in chopped turkey.
6. Place in a large pan with cover and place in fireplace. Dig out ashes and place hot coals on top and bottom of pan. Stir dressing occasionally until done.

Wild Rice Dressing

Amounts	Ingredients
1 pound	wild rice
1 gallon	water
1 tablespoon	salt
1 medium	onion, minced
2	chicken livers
1 quart	chicken broth
1 teaspoon	salt
1 ½ teaspoon	black pepper
1 tablespoon	sage
½ teaspoon	red pepper

Directions

1. Boil rice in water and salt a large black pot with onion and chicken livers.
2. Cool down and stir in remaining ingredients. Cook until desired doneness.

Boiled Kidney Beans

Amounts	Ingredients
1 gallon	water
1	ham hocks, cured
2 cups	kidney beans, picked and washed
1	onion, chopped
1 teaspoon	salt

Directions

1. In a large black pots, boil ham hocks in water until done.
2. Add remaining ingredients, cover and cook for 1 hour.

CHRISTMAS STARCHES

Fried Potatoes

Amounts	Ingredients
2 cups	lard
1 ½ pounds	white potatoes, peeled and quartered
1 teaspoon	salt
1 cup	flour

Directions

1. Heat lard in large black pot heated by wood.
2. Peel, quarter and wash potatoes. Season with salt.
3. Coat potatoes with flour.
4. Fry until crispy in hot lard. Remove from fat and place in serving container.

Rice and Gravy

Amounts	Ingredients
1 cup	Rice
1 ½ cups	water
1 teaspoon	salt

Directions

1. Place rice, water and salt in a large black pot.
2. Boil until rice is fluffy.
3. Set aside.

Brown Gravy

Amounts	Ingredients
1 tablespoon	lard
2 tablespoons	flour
2 cups	water

Directions

1. Heat lard up in skillet. Stir in flour.
2. Cook flour until brown.
3. Gradually stir in water.
4. Stir constantly to prevent lumps.

PRE AND POST SLAVERY REVIEWS

VIRGINIA FORMER SLAVES

Marie Hines
Norfolk, Virginia
Interview taken   March 27, 1937

Cooking

"We cook the white folks vituals on Saturday and lots o' time dey eat cold vituals on Sundays."

Pray Time

"Some of the masters didn't like the way we slaves carried on we would turn pots down and tubs to keep the sound from going out. Den we would have a good time, shouting, singing and praying, just like we pleased."

VIRGINIA TOURIST REGION

SOUTHERN

Cities

1. Danville
2. Emporia
3. South Hill
4. Martinville
5. South Boston
6. Clarksville

Counties

1. Brunswick
2. Buckingham
3. Charlotte
4. Cumberland
5. Greenville
6. Halifax
7. Henry
8. Lunenburg
9. Mecklenburg
10. Pittsylvania

BIBLICAL SCRIPTURES

PSALM 112:1

Praise ye the Lord. Blessed is the man that feareth the Lord.

That delightedly greatly in his commandments.

CHAPTER 9

VEGETABLE COURSES

Possible Recipes That May Have Been Used by Virginia First Slaves

Green Beans with Potatoes

Amounts	Ingredients
3 cups	water
2 strips	salt pork, cut up
1 pound	potatoes
½ teaspoon	red pepper
1 pound	green beans, cut up

Directions

1. In a large black pot, boil water and salt pork until pork is tender.
2. Add and potatoes cook until tender.
3. Stir in red pepper and green beans.
4. Cover and cook for 15 minutes.

Squash Casserole

Amounts	Ingredients
1 pound	yellow squash, chopped
1 teaspoon	salt
1 medium	white onion, chopped
2	eggs, beaten
1 tablespoon	sugar

Directions

1. In a large kettle, boil squash, salt and onion together until tender.
2. Place in a large bowl and stir in remaining ingredients.
3. Place in a baking pan. Bake in pan fireplace until done.

Boiled Lima Beans

Amounts	Ingredients
1 quart	water
1 cured	pig tail
2 cups	lima beans
1 teaspoon	salt

Directions

1. In a medium size black pot, boil pig tails in water until done.
2. Add lima beans and salt. Cover and cook until done.

CHRISTMAS VEGETABLE COURSES

Boiled Mustard Greens

Amounts	Ingredients
1 quart	water
1	ham hock, cured
2 bunches	mustard greens
1	red pepper pod, chopped
1 teaspoon	salt

Directions

1. In a kettle, boil ham hocks until done.
2. Stir in cleaned greens and salt. Add red pepper pod.
3. Cook covered for 30 minutes or until done.

Fried Corn

Amounts	Ingredients
6 ears	corn
1 cup	water
1 tablespoon	butter
1 teaspoon	sugar
1 teaspoon	salt

Directions

1. Clean corn, remove shucks, and silks.
2. Cut the corn three times from cob. Scrape the cob for additional juice.
3. Place butter in a skillet. Melt and add corn to skillet.
4. Stir in sugar and salt. Cook until desired doneness.

Boiled Sweet Potatoes

Amounts	Ingredients
1 pound	sweet potatoes, peeled and cut
2 quarts	water
½ teaspoon	salt
2 tablespoons	butter, melted

Directions

1. Boil sweet potatoes and salt in water in a kettle until soft.
2. Drain water. Mash sweet potatoes. Whip in butter.
3. Serve.

PRE AND POST SLAVERY REVIEWS

VIRGINIA FORMER SLAVES

1. Moble Hopson
   Virginia
   Interview taken at his home in November 28, 1936:
   Born in 1852
   Interviewed by Poquoson River

Parents
"Mammy was an Injun an' muh pappy was uh' white man leastway; he warnt no slave even then he was sorta-dark -skinned.

Coming of the White Man
"Well, de white man come, not fum ober dere. De white man cum cross de Potomac, an' den he cross de York ribber, an' den he cum on cross de Poquoson ribberto dis place. My pappy tell me jas' how dey cross all un close ribbers. He ain't see it, yuh unnerstand but, he hear to tell how it happen.

Well dey across de Potomac an' dey has to fight de Injuns out der until dey kilt all de injuns.

"Dey was kin to de Kink-Ko-tens, but dey had ober on the James de Kink-Ko-tens. When de cross de Poquison dey fine de Injuns, ain't aimes tuh fight but dey kilt de men an' tuk de Injun women fo' dey wives. Course dey warn't no marryin' dem at dat time."

Freedom

"An' when dem Yanks, git here dey aint non of de slave holders as where round. Dey all cleared out an' us blacks is singin' fo' joy cause "Marse Lincoln" done set us free.

'Well, dey tuk de blacks an' dey march us down de turnpike to Hampton an' dey put 'em tuh work at de fort.

Us ain't nevah go ober dere but an heer tell how de black come dere all 'round till dey get so many dey ain't got work fo' us tuh do, so dey got 'em to."

"Yuh wants know why I's put with the colored people fine, I got white skin, least wi, even white white last time I seed it. Well, ah ain't white an he ain't black, leastwise, not so fur as ah know/ What the war done that. Fo de War done warnt no questions come up 'bout it. Ain't been no schools 'round herehere bothup 'both.

Blacks work in de fields, an 'us white own de fields. Dis land here been owned by de Hopsons since us fust Hopson cum here, I guess back fo' de British War, fu' de Injuns war, ah reck'en. Ustuh go tuh de church school wid ole Shep Browns chillum, sat on de same bench, sho did.

"But de war changed all dat. Arter de soljers xome back home, it was diff'rent, first dey say dat all men ain't white, is black."

VIRGINIA TOURIST REGION

NORTHERN VIRGINIA

Cities

1. Alexandria
2. Fairfax
3. Fall Church
4. Fredericksburg
5. Manassas
6. Park
7. Arlington
8. Centraville
9. Chantilly
10. Herndon

11. Clifton
12. Culpepper
13. Leesburg
14. Dulles
15. Manassas Park
16. Marshall
17. McLean
18. Middleburg
19. Occoquan
20. Purcellvile
21. Reston
22. Spotsylvania Spots
23. Springfield
24. Triangle
25. Vienna
26. Warrenton
27. Woodbridge
28. Washington, VA

Counties

1. Clarke
2. Culpepper
3. Fairfax
4. Fauquier
5. King George
6. Loudoun
7. Prince William
8. Rappahannock
9. Spotsylvania
10. Stafford
11. Warren

BIBLICAL SCRIPTURE

Psalm 113:1-3

1 Praise ye Lord. Praise, O ye servants of the Lord, Praise the name of the Lord.

2 Blessed be the name of the Lord from this time forth and for evermore.

3 From the rising of the sun unto the going of the same the Lord's name is to be praised.

CHAPTER 10

BREADS

Possible Recipes May Have Been Used by Virginia First Slaves

THANKSGIVING BREAD

Cornbread Hoe Cakes

Amounts	Ingredients
2 cups	corn meal
1 teaspoon	salt
1 cup	water
2 tablespoons	lard

Directions

1. In a bowl, stir together corn meal, salt and water.
2. Heat lard up in skillet on the fire place.
3. Drop about, 1 tablespoon batter in lard for each cake.
4. Cook until golden brown on each side.

CHRISTMAS BREAD

Hot Water Corn Bread

Amounts	Ingredients
2 cups	corn meal
½ cup	flour
1	egg
2tablespoons	lard
1 cup	hot water

Directions

1. In a bowl, stir together corn meal and flour. Set aside.
2. In a bowl, stir together egg, lard and hog water.
3. Pour into a skillet that has been prepared and cook until done.

PRE AND POST SLAVERY REVIEWS

VIRGINIA FORMER SLAVES

Moble Hopson

Marrying

"An' den dey tell de Injuns' yuh cain't marry no more de whites. Den dey tell men dat an den dey want let us do no bisness wid de whites, so we is th'own in wid de black."

Some of our folks, move away, but dey warn't no use uh movin' cause hear talk et be us some ev'y wher. Do purty soon it come time tuh marry, an' ain't no white women for me to marry so uh marries ah black woman.

An' dat makes me black 'spose cause ah ben livin' black ev'y since.

But mah brother couldn't fine no black woman dat suited him, ah reckon cause he married his first cousin, who was a Hopson humse'f.

"Dem dere only chile hisse'f ah Hopson, and Hopsons been marryin' Hopson ev'y since ah reck'in."

"We can't come no more to church school. An' dey won't let us do bisness with de whites, so we is thrown in wid de blacks."

VIRGINIA TOURIST REGION

Shenandoah Valley

Cities

1. Buena Vista
2. Covington
3. Harrisonburg
4. Lexington
5. Stauton
6. Waynesboro
7. Winchester
8. Shenandoah
9. Luray
10. Front Royal
11. Luray
12. Natural Bridge
13. Berryville

Counties

1. Allegheny
2. Augusta
3. Frederick
4. Warren
5. Clarke
6. Rockbridge, Rockingham,

BIBLICAL SCRIPTURE

PSALM 113:7

He raiseth up the poor out of the dust and lifted up the needy out of the dunghill.

CHAPTER 11

DESSERT COURSE

Possible Recipes May Have **Been** Used by Virginia First Slaves

THANKSGIVING DESSERTS

Sweet Potato Custard

Amounts	Ingredients
1 pound	sweet potatoes, cooked
1 cup	sugar
1 cup	molasses
1 teaspoon	salt
2	eggs, beaten
1 cup	cream

Directions

1. In a bowl, beat together all ingredients.
2. Place in a large skillet. Cover and bake until done.

Molasses Cake

Amounts	Ingredients
2 cups	flour
1 teaspoon	salt
1 teaspoon	soda
1 cup	molasses
1 cup	buttermilk
3	eggs, beaten

Directions

1. Stir together flour, salt and soda. Set aside.
2. In a separate bowl, stir together molasses, buttermilk and eggs.
3. Whip together flour mixture and buttermilk mixture.
4. Place into a greased pan and place cover on top and bake in fireplace until done.

Buttermilk Pie

Amounts	Ingredients
2 cups	buttermilk
1 cup	sugar
1	eggs, beaten
½ cup	molasses

Pie Crust

2 cups	flour
1 teaspoon	salt
½ cup	lard
½ cup	water

Directions

For crust

1. In a bowl, stir together flour and salt.
2. Use a fork and stir in lard.
3. Gradually add water. Make into a ball.
4. Press out ball in the bottom of a pan.

For Pie.

1. In a bowl, mix together buttermilk with remaining ingredients.
2. Pour into prepared pie crust.
3. Bake in fireplace until done.

Molasses Pie

Amounts	Ingredients
2 cups	molasses
1 cup	pecans, chopped
1 cup	butter, soften
1	eggs, beaten

Directions

1. Mix all ingredients together and set aside.
2. Prepare pie crust.

Pie Crust

Amounts	Ingredients
2 cups	self rising flour
½ cups	pecans, chopped
1 cup	butter
½ cup	water

Directions

1. Mix together flour and pecans.
2. Chop in butter.
3. Gradually add water.
4. Make into a ball.
5. Using your hand, pat crust out evenly

In the bottom of a skillet. Make holes in the crust and bake for 15 minutes.

6. Remove from heat, pour molasses mixture over crust and cook for 30 minutes.

CHRISTMAS DESSERTS

Apple Cobbler

Amounts	Ingredients
4 cups	apples, sliced
1 cup	brown sugar
1 teaspoon	salt
2 tablespoons	flour
¼ cup	butter, soften

Cobbler Topping

2 cups	flour
½ cup	butter
1 teaspoon	salt
½ cup	water

Directions

1. In a bowl, combine apples brown sugar, salt, flour and butter.
2. Stir well. Set aside.

For Cobbler Top Crust

1. In a separate bowl, stir together all pie crust ingredients.
2. Pat out into a large circle.

For Cobbler

1. Use a large black skillet, pour apple mixture in the bottom.
2. Smooth out pie crust on top.
3. Bake for 1 hour in fireplace.
4. Sprinkle sugar on top.

Pumpkin Pie

Amounts	Ingredients
4 cups	pumpkin, cooked and mashed
1 cup	milk
1 ½ cups	brown sugar
½ cup	butter, melted
2	eggs, beaten

Directions

1. In a bowl, mix all ingredients together.
2. Set aside and make crust.

Pie Crust

Amounts	Ingredients
3 cups	flour
1 teaspoon	salt
1 ½ cups	lard
½ cup	water

Directions

1. In a bowl, mix together flour, salt and lard.
2. Gradually add in water.
3. Make a large circle with the crust and place in bottom of a large skillet.
4. Pour pumpkin mixture on top of crust and bake for 40 minutes.

PRE- AND POST SLAVERY REVIEWS

VIRGINIA FORMER SLAVES

Albert Jones
Civil War Veteran
Age 95 years
Portsmouth, Virginia
Interviewed in January,1937 by Thelma Dunston

Born

Born a slave in. South Hampton County. Worked as a house boy.

Civil War

"When I was a twenty-one, me and one of my brothers run away to fight with the Yankees. Us left South Hampton County and went to Petersburg. Dere we got some food."

Den we went to Fort Hatten County where we met some more slaves who had done run away. When we got in Fort Hatten, we had to cross a bridge to git to de Yankees. De rebels had torn de bridge down. We all go together and build back de bridge to get to de Yankees. Wewent to de Yankees. De give us food and clothes. Den us left Souf Hampton County and went to Petersburg.

Civil War Uniform

"The uniform dat I wor wuz blue wif brass buttons: a blue caps, lined wif red flannel black leather boots and a blue cap. I rode on a bay color horse – fast everybody on Company "E" had bay color horse. I tooked my knap-sack and blanket on de horse back. In my knap sack, I had water, hard tack and other foods."

Women in the Civil War

"Not only wus dere men slaves run to de Yankees, but some un de women slaves followed dere husbands. Dey use to help washing and cooking."

War Ended

"When de war ended, I goes back to my mastah, and he treated me like his brother. Guess he Was scared of me 'cause I had so much ammunition on me. My brother who went wif me to de Yankees caught rheumatism doing de war. He died after de war ended."

VIRGINIA TOURIST REGION

West Central

Cities

1. Bedford
2. Lynchburg
3. Radford
4. Roanoke
5. Salem

Counties

1. Albermarle
2. Amelia
3. Amherst County
4. Appomattox
5. BuckinghamCambell
6. Chesterfield
7. Dinwiddie
8. Fluvanna
9. Greene Henrico
10. Hanover
11. Louisia
12. Madison
13. Nelsia
14. Notbway

15. Orange
16. Powhotan
17. Prince Edward
18. Prince George
19. Sussex

BIBLICAL SCRIPTURE

PSALM 115:1

I love the Lord because he hath heard my voice and my Supplications.

CHAPTER 12

BEVERAGE COURSE

Possible Recipes Used by Virginia First Slaves

Buttermilk

Amounts	Ingredients
2 quarts	sour cream

Directions

1. Churn the cream until butter is made.
2. Skim the butter from the milk.
3. The left over milk is called buttermilk.

Coffee

Amounts	Ingredients
1 cup	coffee beans, chopped and browned
4 cups	water

Directions

1. Place all ingredients in a kettle and then boil for 30 minutes in the fireplace.
2. Cook until desired consistency.

Apple Cider

Amounts	Ingredients
1 gallon	apple juice, ground from apples

Directions

Corn Shuck Tea

Amounts	Ingredients
5	corn shucks, brown, cured
1 gallon	water
1 cup	honey

Directions

1. Boil corn shucks in water in a large kettle.
2. Strain tea.
3. Cool and stir in honey.
4. Serve

Eggnog

Amounts	Ingredients
1 gallon	sweet milk
3	eggs, beaten
2 cups	sugar
1	vanilla bean

Directions

1. In a large pan, beat all ingredients together.
2. Pour into large kettle and cook on low heat for ten minutes.
3. Cool and serve.

PRE AND POST SLAVERY REVIEWS

VIRGINIA FORMER SLAVES

Susan Kelley, 100 years
Simon Stokes, 100 years
Guinea, Virginia
Interview by George W. Billups

Susan Kelly

"Mother -Anna Birrellel, was slave to Col. Hayes.:

Ash Cakes

"Mammy used her baked ash-cakes; dey wuz made wid meal, with a little salt and mixed wid water; den mammy would rake up de ashed in de fire- places den she would mak up de meal in round cakes, and put dem in de hot bricks ter bake. When dey had cooked round de edges, she would put ashes on de top ob dem, when dey wuz nice and brown and she took dem out and wash dem off wid water."

Simon Stokes

Simon Stokes, son of Kit and Anna Stokes and family parents were slaves later moved to Gloucester County, and bought a farm near Gloucester Point.

"In de fall when de simmons wuz ripe, me and de odder boys who had a big time possum huntin' time all would git two or three a night; and we all would put down up and feed dem hoe-cake and simmons fer git dem nice and fat; den mammy would roast dem with sweet taters round them. Dey wuz sho' good, all roasted nice and brown with sweet taters in de graby."

BIBLICAL SCRIPTURE

PSALM 117:1

O praise the Lord all ye nations: Praise him, all ye people.

For his merciful kindness is great toward us: and the truth of the Lord endureth for ever. Praise ye the Lord.

CHAPTER 13

SNACKS

Possible Recipes Used by Virginia First Slaves

THANKSGIVING SNACKS

Roasted Peanuts

Amounts	Ingredients
1 pound	guber peanuts, in shell, cured

Directions

1. Place peanuts in a large skillet
2. Put skillet in the fireplace over low coals.
3. Roast for 30 minutes. Stir constantly.

Hickory Nuts Cookies

Amounts	Ingredients
2 cups	flour
1 teaspoon	salt
1 teaspoon	soda
1 cup	butter
1 cup	sugar
2	egg, beaten
½ cup	hickory nuts, chopped

Amounts Ingredients

1. Stir together flour, salt and soda. Set aside.
2. Stir together butter, sugar and beaten egg.

3. Stir together flour mixture and butter mixture.
4. Stir in hickory nuts.
5. Pat out into 18 cookies.
6. Bake in skillet in fireplace.

Smoked Crab Legs

Amounts	Ingredients
2 pounds	crab legs, washed and cleaned.

Directions

1. Build a pit about 4 X 4 and fill with hickory chips. Make fire with chips.
2. Place wire over hot hickory chips. Place Crab legs on top of wire and cook for 10 minutes. Turn frequently.
3. Serve hot.

Syrup Candy

Amounts	Ingredients
1 cup	molasses
1 cup	brown sugar
½ teaspoon	salt
1 teaspoon	soda
1 cup	whole pecans

Directions

1. In a black pot stir together molasses, brown sugar and salt.
2. Bring to a boil and stir constantly for 30 minutes.
3. Add soda. Stir very fast.
4. Cook for 15 minutes and add pecans halves.
5. Cool and dip out with spoon and make 25 pieces.

CHRISTMAS SNACKS

Dried Shrimp

Amounts	Ingredients
2 pounds	shrimp
1 tablespoon	salt

Directions

1. Wash shrimp and sprinkle with salt.
2. Thread shrimp on 10 long sticks made from tree branches.
3. Smoke shrimp until dried.

Dried Apricots

Amounts	Ingredients
1 pound	apricots, fresh, washed and seeds removed.

Directions

1. Wash and remove seeds.
2. Place on top of clean cheese cloth.
3. Dry in sun. Turn every day.

Pickled Pig's Feet

Amounts	Ingredients
6	pig's feet, halved, cleaned
2 tablespoons	salt
1 gallon	water
1 gallon	apple cider vinegar
2 pods	red pepper, sliced

Directions

1. In a big black pot, cook pig feet halves with salt in water until tender.
2. Destroy water. Heat pig feet in vinegar with pepper pods for 15 minutes.
3. Let stand three hours. Serve.

Baked Sweet Potatoes in Ashes

Amounts	Ingredients
6	Sweet potatoes
6	collard green leaves

Directions

1. Make hot ashes in fireplace.
2. Wash sweet potatoes. Set Aside.
   Wash collard green leaves.
3. Tightly wrap each sweet potatoe in the collard greens.
4. Place sweet potatoes wrapped in collard greens in fireplace and cover with ashes.
5. Bake for one hour or until potatoes are done.
6. Wash off ashes and remove collard green leaf.
7. Serve with butter.

PRE AND POST SLAVERY REVIEWS

VIRGINIA FORMER SLAVES

1. Richard Slaughter
   Hampton, Virginia
   December 27, 1936
   Born: January 9, 1849
   Place called Epps Island, City Point, I was born a slave"
   Owner name was Dr. Richard J. Epps

Left at age 13 or 14 years Hampton was already burnt when I came here. I came to Hampton in 1868. The Yankees burned Hampton and the fleet went up the James River. My father and mother and cousins went abroad the Meritana with me. You see, my father and three or four men left in the darkness and got aboard. Thegun boats would fire on the towns and plantations and run the white folks off. After that they would carry all the colored folks off. After that they would carry all the colored folks back down here to Old Point and put them behind enemy line.

Spanish America War

"That was during the McKinley time. He went down the Texas and some of them other ships gave Puerto Rico Hail Columbia.

They blew up the Maine with a mine. She was blown up inward. The Maine left Hampton Road going toward Savannah when they looked at what was left of here all the steel was bent inward which shows that she was blown up from the outside in.

While I was there, wus the hanging of three Mexicans for themurder of a soldier.

In September, we left Brownville and come back to Baltimore. Before. Before this I was sent up the Rio Grande. Barracks as boss cook. I then returned to Hampton and I lived as an oysterman and fisherman for over 40 years. I have never been wounded. My clothes have been cut off me by bullets but Lord kept them off my back, I guess.

Slaves Run Away

"Did slaves ever run away! Lord, yes where I was born there is a lots of water. Why there used to be a high as ten and twelve Dutch three masters in the labor at a time. I used to catch little snakes and other things like terrapin, and selling 'em to the sailor for to eat roaches on the ship. In those days a good captain around had a slave up in the top rail carry him out of Virginia to New York and Yankees."

Abraham Lincoln

"I knew the names of all the gunboats that came up the river. There was the Galena, we called him the old cheese box. The Delaware, the Yankee, the Meeker and the Meritana, which was the ship I was board of. That year the Merrimas and monitor fought off.

I came to Hampton as a water boy. While I was aboard the gunboat, they captured a rebel gunboat at a place called Drary's Bluff.

When I first came to Hampton, there were only barracks where theinstitute is, when I returned General Armstrong had done rite smart.

"I left Hampton stillas a waterboy and went byGivre Creek, Bellvine, Va. A place near Harper's Ferry. I left the Creek aboard a steamer, the General Hookery and went to Alesandria, Va. Abraham Lincoln came aboard the ship and we carried him to

Mt. Vernon, George Washington old home. What did he look like. Why, he looked more like an old preacher then anything I know.

"Have you ever seen any picture of him? Well, if, you have seen a picture of him, you seen him. He just like the picture.

Colored Troops

"No I never went to what you call school except to school as a soldier. I went to Baltimore in 1864 and enlisted. I was about 17 years then. My officers' names were Capt. Joe Reed, Lieutenant as Stinson, and Colonel Joseph Perkins. I was assigned to the Nineteenth Regiment of Maryland Company A. WI was in training, they fought at Petersburg I went to the regiment in '64 and stayed in until I was a cook. They taken Richmond the fifth day of April 1865. On that day I walked up the road to Richmond.

"When we left Richmond, my brigdade was ordered to Brownsville, Texas. We went there the way of Old Point Comfort, where was aboard a transport.

When we got to Brownsville, I was detailed to a hospital staff. We arrived in Brownsville in January 1867

2. Elizabeth Sparks
    Mathews Court House
    Virginia
    Interviewed by Claude Anderson; January 13, 1937

    Childhood
    -For dinner, they ate ash cakes baked on the blade of a hoe.
    -Lived at Sandford given as a 'wedding present' to Master's daughter.
    -Lived in Springdale

Civil War
Slaves knew what the war was 'bout. After the war, they tried to fool the slaves 'bout freedom an' wanted to keep 'em on a workin' but the Yankees told 'em they were free.

They sent some of the slaves to South Carolina. When the Yankees came near to keep the Yankees from gittin' 'em.

I nevah will forgit when the Yankees came through.

They wuz takin' all the livestock an' all the men slaves back to Norfolk, wid 'em to break up the system. White folks head wus jes' goin' to keep on havin' slaves. The slaves wanted freedom, but the's scared to tell the white folks so, Anyway the Yankees wuz givin' everythin' to the slave.

Rations in Virginia

"Women with children -1/2 bushel of cornmeal a week

-Childless women -1 peck of meal

Favored Girl Slave

Slave girl Betty Lilly always had good clothes an' all the privileges. She was favorite of his. We uster sing a song when he was shippin' the slaves sell 'em 'bout "Massa Gwyne Sell Us Tomorrow."

3. Mary Jane Wilson
    Portsmouth, Virginia
    Interview by: Thelma Dunston

Freedom

"My father went to work in the Norfolk Navy Yardd as a teamster. He began right away buying us a home. He was one of the first Negro-land owners in Portsmouth after Emancipation.

After Emancipation

After Emancipation, father built a school for her in the backyard held graduation in EMANUEL A.M.E CHURCH.

VIRGINIA TOURIST REGION

CHESAPEAKE BAY

Cities

1. Kilmarnock
2. Warsaw
3. Urbana
4. West Point
5. Colonial Beach
6. Tappachannock
7. Gloucester
8. Irvington

Counties

1. Middlesex County
2. Lancaster County
3. Northern Gerland County

4. Richmond County
5. King William County
6. King and Queen County
7. Mathews County
8. Westmoreland County
9. Essex County
10. Gloucester County
11. King George County

PSALM 118: 5

I called upon the Lord in distress: The Lord answered me; and set me in a large place.

PART II

MARYLAND

CHAPTER 14

Slaves came to Maryland with English settlers. They arrived on the Atlantic Ocean in the Tidewater region.

There were two types of slaves the house slaves and the field slaves. The House slaves, sometimes called the house servants, prepared food for their owners and ate the same foods as their owners. They ate the leftovers from the owners' table. The field slaves would prepare their meals in the fields, outside or inside of the slaves' cabins.

FOODS RESOURCES THAT MAY HAVE BEEN AVAILABLE FOR FIRST THANKSGIVING AND CHRISTMAS DINNERS MADE BY FIRST SLAVES OF MARYLAND

(Note: In 1863, President Abraham Lincoln signed a proclamation of a national Thanksgiving Day last Thursday of November, a day of Thanksgiving to our Father who dwelleth in Heaven.)

TYPES OF FOOD	SOURCES
1. Meats	Plantations, wildlife, Freshwater and ocean Indians
2. Flour, Corn,	Plantations, Indians
3. Sugar, Molasses	Ship, Slave Trade
4. Dried Beans, Peas, Rice and wild rice	Slave Ship
5. Vegetables, fresh, okra	Indians
6. Field peas, corn, yams, meal, goober peanuts, salt fish, kola nuts -Slave ship	
7. Wild animals and poultry	Indians
8. Dairy, Eggs	Slave owners
9. Seasonings, salt Sea Salt, herb	Slave trade,

10.	Wild fruits apples, pears, Peaches, berries	Indians
11	Lard	plantation
12	Water, fresh	Plantation springs
13	Cinnamon, vanilla, black pepper	Slave braids

Slaves would braid seeds in their hair
For their private seasonings

Food Cooking

1.	Heat Source	wood, hickory, rocks
2.	Black pots, fireplaces	slave holders, Indians
3.	Cooking utensils	slaves constructions
		From trees, gourds and sea shells
4.	Eating troughs	plantation
5.	Tables	Slaves constructions
6.	Eating utensils	sea shells and slave constructions
		Of eating utensils; or hands used
		For eating -finger foods
7.	Food measurements slaves	estimation of ingredients

ABOUT MARYLAND

(MD)
OLD LINE, FREE STATE
(Slave state from 1788 until 1865)

Capital   Annapolis

History: Capitan John Smith, first explored Maryland in 1608. William Claiborne set up a trading post on Kent Island in Chesapeake Bay 1631. Britain granted land to Cecilus Calvert Lord Baltimore, 1637, his brother led 200 settlers to St. Mary's River,1634 The bravery of Maryland troops in the Revolution as at the Battle of Long Island, won the state its nickname, The Old Line State. In the War of 1812, when a British fleet tried to take Fort McHenry Marylander, Francis Scott Key 1814, wrote The Star Spangled Banner

STATE DATA:		
	Motto:	Fatti Maschi, Parole Femine (Manly deeds, womanly Words)
	Flower:	Black-eyed Susan
	Bird:	Baltimore Oriole
	Tree:	White Oak
	Song:	Maryland, My Maryland
	Entered Union:	Seventh of the original 13 states
		To ratify Constitution, April 28, 1788
	People:	Racial distribution: White (major ethnic Group German, Italian, Russian, English, Polish), Blacks, Hispanics
	Geography:	Total area:10,577 square miles,
	Rank:	42
	Land area:	9,891 square miles, Acres forested land: 2,652, 200
	Location:	Middle Atlantic state stretching from the ocean To the Allegheny Mountains.

Climate:	Continental in the west: humid subtropical in the east.
Topography:	Eastern Shores of coastal plain and Piedmont Plateau, and the Blue Ridge, separated by the Chesapeake Bay.
Principal Industries:	Food, manufacturing, tourism
Principal Manufactured goods:	Food and kindred products, primary Metals; electrics and electronic Equipment
Agriculture:	Chief crops: tobacco, corn, soybeans
Livestock:	cattle pigs/pigs/ sheep, poultry
Lumber/timber:	Hardwoods
Minerals:	coal, sand, stone and gravel
Chief Ports:	Baltimore International
Airport:	Baltimore
Tourist attractions:	Racing events include the Preakness at Pimilico track, Baltimore, the International at Laurel Race Course, the John B. Campbell Handicap at Bowie; restored Fort McHenry; Baltimore, near which Frances Scott Key wrote the Star Spangled, Antietam Battlefield, 1862, near Hagertown, South Mountain Battlefield, 1862; Edgar Allan Poe home, Baltimore, The State House, Annapolis, 1772, the oldest still in use in the U.S.
Famous Marylanders:	Benjamin Banneker; Francis Scott Key First African Slaves

Harriet Tubman, born in Maryland-1823-1913 -Underground Railroad Conductor; The Underground Railroad was not a railway but a way for slaves to escape from the plantation system served as a nurse and spy for Union Army in the Civil War.

The Underground Railroad was said to begin after the Revolutionary War. However, the term was begun by a slave owner when his slave, Tico Davids, a slave, swam the

The Ohio River and escaped slavery.

- Frederick Douglas-abolishistionist

Regions of Maryland

Maryland has five Regions

1. Western Region
2. Capitol Region
3. Central Region
4. Southern Region
5. Eastern Shore Region

Mason-Dixon Line

The Mason-Dixon Line in Maryland. The Line was known for dividing slave states and the free state.

PRE AND POST SLAVERY REVIEWS

MARYLAND INFORMANTS
Maryland   Volume 8
Former Slaves and Addresses After Emancipations

1. Lucy Brown   1
    Montgomery County
    Forest Glen, Maryland

2. Charles Coles   4
    1106 Sterling St.
    Baltimore, Maryland

3. James V. Deane   8
    Baltimore, Maryland

4. Mrs. M. S. Fayman   10
    Cherry Heights
    Baltimore, Maryland

5. Thomas Foote   14
    Cockeysville, Maryland

6. Menelis Gussmany   17
    Baltimore, Maryland

7. Caroline Hammond   22
    Baltimore, Maryland

8. Page Harris
    Camp Parole, Maryland

BIBLICAL SCRIPTURES:

PSALM 107:4-6

4 They wandered in the wilderness in a solitary way: they found no city to dwell in.

5 Hungry and thirsty their soul fainted in them;

6 Then they cried unto the Lord in their troubles and he delivered them out of their distresses.

CHAPTER 15

Two Possible Thanksgiving and Snacks Menus May Have
Been Used By the Maryland First African Slaves

Thanksgiving Menus

I

Shrimp and FuFu
Deviled Eggs

Hot Pepper Soup
Goat Head Soup

Roasted Turkey
Fish Boil
Cornbread Stuffing
Jollof Rice
Boiled Collard Greens/ Cured Meat
Succotash
Cracklin' Bread
Hush Puppies
Berry Cobbler
Sweet Potato Pie

Snacks
Fried Pork Chop/Biscuit Sandwich
Fried Pork Skins

II

Maryland Crab Cakes
Fried Plantains
Pumpkin Stew
White Potato Soup

Roasted Rack of Goat
Chicken and Dumplings
Fried Eggplant

Mustard Greens, hot peppers
Chow Chow

Egg Bread
Hoecakes

Egg Custard Pie
Peach Cobbler

Snacks
Cane Syrup Cookies
Souse Meat

PRE-AND POST SLAVERY REVIEW

1. Lucy Brooks
   Forest Glen

   (Lives in a shack with her son in the Carrol Springs Property of Forrest Glen.)

   Interviewer: Guthrie

   Born: Born on the Bay on the Severn Riverin Maryland 15th day, October.

   Belonged to Misses Ann Garner. She owned 75 slaves she hadn't sold when the war ended.

   Food on the Plantation: I hab mostly clabber milk, fish and corn bread. We gots plenty of fish down on the bay.

2. Charles Coles
   Baltimore

   11/16/37

   Interviewer: Rogers

   Born: About 1861, part of Charles County

   "I do not know who my parents were nor my relatives lived by a slave member who was a fine Christian gentlemen as a member of the catholic church.

   Plantation size3500 acres. Work time 7 am to 6:00p.m.

   Slave Funerals: The slave funerals on Dorsey plantation was conducted by a priest. The corpse was buried in the Dorseys' graveyard, a lot of about 1 ½ acres, surrounded by cedar trees and well cared for.

   The only differences in the graves, that the Dorsey people had marble markers and the slaves had plain stones.

   Church: I am still Catholic and will always be a member of St. Peter Clavier Church.

3. James V. Deane
   Baltimore, Maryland

   Born at Goose Bay in Chester County, May 30, 1857.

   Born to slave parents -John and Jane Deane.

   Born on the Potomac River.

   Size of Plantation: 10,000 acres

Work as a child: As a slave, I worked on the farm with small boys-thinning corn, watching watermelon patches and later I worked in wheat and tobacco fields.

Slave Sold:

Only one slave sold from the plantation she was my aunt, the mistresses slapped her one day. She struck back. She was sold and taken down south.

We never saw her or heard from her afterwards.

Slave Marriages

He had seen. The master held the broom handle for the groom jumping over it as a part of a wedding ceremony. When a slave married someone from another plantation, the master of the wife owning all the children. For the wedding the ordinary clothes, sometimes you could not tell the original outfit for the patches, and sometimes Kentucky jeans.

Supper and Cornshuckings

Had at 12 o'clock at right menu roast pig, apple sauce, honey and corn bread

Singing

"When we wanted to meet at night. We would meet on the bank of the Potomac River and sing across the river to the slaves in Virginia and They sing back to us."

BIBLICAL SCRIPTURES

PSALM 107:7-9

7 And he led them forth by the right way, that they might go to the city of habitation.

8 Oh that men would praise the Lord for his goodness, and for his wonderful works the children of men?

9 For he satisfieth the longing soul, and filleth the hungry soul with goodness.

CHAPTER 16

Two Possible Christmas and Snack Menus
Maryland's First African Slaves
May Have Used

Christmas Menus

I

Applesauce
Fried Chicken Livers
Okra Soup
Sweet Potato Soup
Maryland Ham -Fried
Boiled Chitterlings/ Rice
Corn Pudding
Boiled Kale Greens
Boiled Butter Beans

Spoon Bread
Sweet Potato Pudding
Vinegar Pie

Peach Brandy
Snacks
Tea Cakes
Pecan Pralines

II

Cabbage Stew
Opossum Stew
Chicken Pot Pie
Oxtails and Rice

Skillet Cornbread

Ash Cakes (the ash cakes in Maryland were baked in the ashes in the fire place or camp fire in wrap one of the following wet leaves, such as, corn shucks, cabbage leaves, collard green leaves or poplar leaves. Bake each ash cake for about 15 minutes.)

Pound Cake

Jelly Cake

Snacks

Peanut Brittle

Fried Corn Pops

PRE- AND POST SLAVE REVIEWS

1. Thomas Foote
    Cockeysville, Maryland
    (A Free Negro)
    Interview Date: 1937

    "My mother's master's name was Myers, a daughter of a free man of Baltimore)

    Member of the Masonic Lodge and belong to Odd Fellows at Towson, Maryland.

2. Mrs. M.S. Fayman
    Baltimore, Maryland

    "I was born in St. Nuzare Paris in Louisiana 60 miles south of Baton Rouge, in 1850.

"Spoke French-went to French Schools in Baton Rouge, conducted by French Sisters.

"Taught French to the children of Pierce Buckson Hughes will known slave trader and plantation owner in Kentucky."

BIBLICAL SCRIPTURES

PSALM 107:12-15

12 Therefore, he brought down their heart with labour: they fell down and their was none to help.

13 Then they cried unto the Lord in their trouble, and he saved them out of their distresses.

14 He brought them out of darkness and the shadow of death, and brake their

Hands in sunder.

15 Oh that men would Praise the Lord for his goodness, and for his wonderful works in the children of men!

CHAPTER 17

APPETIZERS COURSE

Possible Recipes That May Have Used by the First African Slaves of Maryland for Appetizers

APPETIZERS RECIPES

Shrimp/FuFu

Amounts	Ingredients
1 pound	shrimp, deveined and cleaned
1 teaspoon	salt
¼ cup	butter, softened

Directions

1. Clean and wash shrimp. Pat dry.
2. Season with salt
3. Melt butter in iron skillet heated over hot coals.
4. Stir in shrimp and cook for 5 minutes.
5. Serve over fufu

To make Fufu:

Amounts	Ingredients
½ pound	white corn kernels
1 tablespoon	salt
2 cups	water, boiling

1. Grind or pound white corn kernels to thin meal. Place in a bowl.
2. Stir in salt.
3. Heat water in a black skillet over hot coals.

4. Stir in cornmeal mixture and cook for 15 minutes or until desired doneness.
5. Place cooked corn meal on plate and place cooked shrimp on top of corn meal mixture.

Deviled Eggs

Amounts	Ingredients
12	eggs
1 gallon	water
½ cup	vinegar
1 teaspoon	salt
¼ cup	onion, minced
¼ cup	chow chow

Directions

1. Place eggs and water in a large black pot and cook over hot coals.
2. Cook until done. Cool eggs and peel. Half eggs and place yolks in a bowl.
3. Save egg whites until later.
4. Mash egg yolks and whip in remaining ingredients.
5. Divide egg yolk mixture into egg whites. Serve.

Maryland Crab Cakes

Amounts	Ingredients
2 pounds	crabmeat, picked and chopped
2	eggs, beaten
1 teaspoon	salt
½ teaspoon	black pepper
¼ cup	onion, minced
1 cup	flour
1 ½ cups	lard

Directions

1. Wash and clean crab legs. Place picked crab legs in a bowl
2. Stir in all ingredients except flour and lard.
3. Make crab mixture into 8 patties. Roll each patty in flour.
4. Heat lard in black skillet over hot coals.
5. Fry each crab patty in hot lard until golden brown.

Fried Plantains

Amounts	Ingredients
4	plantains, peeled and cut into chips
	Cut into chips
4 cups	lard
1 tablespoon	salt

Directions

1. Peel and plantains. Slice into chips.
2. Heat lard in a pan over hot coals.
3. Fry plantains until golden brown.
4. Remove from hot lard.
5. Place on plate and sprinkle with salt.

Applesauce

Amounts	Ingredients
2 pounds	apples, peeled, cored and quartered
	Water to cover
1 cup	sugar

Directions

1. Peel and pare apples.
2. Place apples and water in a big black pot and cook over hot coals.
3. Cook until apples are soft. Remove from pot. Mash apples and add Sugar.

4. Cool and serve about ½ cup to each guest.

Fried Chicken Livers

Amounts	Ingredients
1 pound	chicken livers, cleaned and washed
1 teaspoon	salt
2 cups	flour
2 cups	lard

Directions

1. Clean and wash livers.
2. Season with salt.
3. Roll each chicken liver in flour, until well coated.
4. Heat lard very hot in a heavy black skillet over hot coals.

PRE AND POST SLAVE REVIEWS

1. Menellis Gassaway
   Carrollton Avenue
   Baltimore, Maryland
   Date of Interview: Sept 13, 1937
   Born in Freedom District Carroll County, about 1850 or 52.

   Parents

   "My father was owned by a man name of Mr. Dorsey. My mother was bound out by Mr. Dorsey to a man by the name of Mr. Norris of Frederick County.

2. Caroline Hammond
   4710 Falls Road
   Baltimore, Maryland

Born in Anne Arundel County near Davidsonville about 3 miles from South River in the year 1844. She was a daughter of a freeman and a slave woman.

She was 95 years old.

Special Mother -High Social Standing in Annapolis, Maryland

"Exception of several of the household help who ate and slept in the manor house. My mother being one of the household slaves, enjoyed certain Privileges that the farm slaves did not. She was the head cook of Mr. Davidson household. The Davidson's and his family were considered people of high social standing in Annapolis.)

High Status

Mr. Davidson and his family were considered people of high social standing in Annapolis and the people in the county. Mr. Davidson's entertained on a large scale, especially many of the officers of the Naval Academy and Annapolis and his friends in Baltimore. Mrs. Davidson's dishes were finest terrapin and Maryland's finest wines and champagne.

Table Service

"All of the cooking was supervised by my mother and the table was waited on by Uncle Billie, dressed in a uniform, decorated with brass buttons, in a funny vest, his hands encased in white gloves."

3. Page Harris
   Camp Parole, Maryland
   "Born in 1859 or 1860."

I was born in 1858 about 2 miles west of Chicamaxen near the Potomac River in Charles County in the farm of Boston Stafford better known as Blood Hound Manor. This name was applied because Mr. Stafford raised and trained blood hounds to track

Runaway slaves and to sell to slaveholders of Maryland, Virginia and other southern states as far as Mississippi and Louisiana."

4. Annie Young Hinson
    Baltimore
    Born in Northumberland County, Virginia
    85 years old, owned by Doctor Presley

"The food consisted of beef, hog meat and lamb and mutton and of the vegetables raised on the farm.

"I remember well that day that Dr. Bellum, just as if it were yesterday, that we went to the court house to be set free. Bellum walked in front 65 of us behind him walked in front of us behind him. When we got there the sheriff asked him if they were his slaves. The Dr. said they were but not now, after the papers were signed we all went back to the plantation. Some stayed there, others went away. I came to Baltimore and I have never been back since. I think I was about 17 or 18 years old."

5. Rev. Silas Jackson
    Baltimore, Maryland
    Born in Ashbie's Gap in Virginia in the year of 1846 or 47-90 years. Mother and father purchased by my master from trader in Richmond, Virginia.

"The only things I know about my grandparents were: My grandfather ran away through the aid of Harriet Tubman and went to Philadelphia and save $350 to purchased by grandmother through the aid of a quaker or an Episcopal minister. I do not know."

"Our food were cooked by our mothers and sisters and for those who were not married by the old women and men as signed for that work."

"On New Year's Day we all were scared, that was the time for selling, buying and trading slaves. We did not know who was to go or come."

6. James Calhart James
   At home 2450 Druid Holl Avenue
   Baltimore, Maryland
   "Born August 23, 1846. The son of the Confederate and daughter of the Indian, my masters slave woman." My master was my father. Bought to Maryland from Virginia.

Freedom

"An de blowing and the beating of de drums. When General Sherman comes no more we will hear no more crying. Old master will be alright."

BIBLICAL SCRIPTURES

PSALM 107:25-28

25 For he commandeth, and raiseth the stormy wind, which lifteth up the waves thereof.

26 They mount up to the heaven they go down again to the depths: their soul is melted because of trouble.

27 They reel to and fro and stagger like a drunken man, and are at their wits end.

28 Then they cry unto the Lord in their trouble, and he bringeth them out of their distresses.

CHAPTER 18

SOUP AND STEW COURSES

Possible Recipes That May Have Been Used by the First African Slaves of Maryland for Soups and Stews

Soups and Stews Recipes:

Pumpkin Stew

Amounts	Ingredients
4 cups	water
2	chicken thighs, washed and chopped
1 teaspoon	salt
½ cup	onion, minced
4 cups	pumpkin, cubed
2 tablespoons	butter
½ cup	brown sugar
1 pod	green pepper, chopped

Direction

1. In a large black pot heated over hot coals, cook chicken thighs in water until tender. Covered.
2. Stir in salt and onion. Continue to cook.
   Add pumpkin cubes, cover and cook for 30 minutes.
3. Stir in remaining ingredients. Cover and cook over low heat for 45 minutes.

White Potato Soup

Amounts	Ingredients
1 pound	white potatoes, cubed
	Water to cover
2 tablespoons	lard
2 teaspoons	salt
2 cups	milk
2 tablespoons	butter

Directions

1. Peel and wash potatoes.
2. Add potatoes and water to cover to a large black pot. Cover. Cook over hot coals until potatoes are soft and done.
3. Add remaining ingredients; cover.
4. Cook for 45 minutes. Stir constantly.

Okra Soup

Amounts	Ingredients
1	fryer chicken, cut up
	water to cover
2	onions, chopped
2 pounds	okra, chopped
2 cups	sweet potatoes, cubed
2 teaspoons	salt

Directions

1. Clean and wash chicken. Place
Chicken and water to cover in a large
Black pot heat over hot coals. Cover and
Bring to boil. Cook until tender.

2. Add remaining ingredients. Stir and cook over low heat until tender.

Sweet Potato Soup

Amounts	Ingredients
1 cured	pig's tail chopped
	Water to cover
4 cups	sweet potatoes, chopped
½ cup	onion, chopped
1 teaspoon	salt
2 tablespoons	sugar
1 pint	milk

Directions

1. Place pig's tail and water in a big black pot
   Until tender.
2. Add remaining ingredients, except milk,
   Cook covered until sweet potatoes are tender.
3. Stir in milk and cook uncovered until
   Desired doneness.

Hot Pepper Soup

Amounts	Ingredients
1	chicken, cut up
1 gallon	water
2	yellow onions,
Chopped	
1 pound	white potato, cubed
½ cup	green hot peppers, chopped
2 teaspoons	salt

Directions

1. In a large black pot, place chicken and water and onions. Cook covered over hot coals until chicken is tender.
2. Stir in remaining ingredients and cover.
3. Cook over low heat until desired doneness.

Goat Head Soup

Amounts	Ingredients
1	goat's head, cleaned and washed
2 gallons	water
¼ cup	salt
2 medium	onions, chopped
2 pods	hot peppers, chopped
2 cups	rice

Directions

1. Clean and wash goat head. Place in water. Add salt and onion. Cook in a large black pot and cover. Cook over hot Coals until tender.
2. Stir in rice and hot pepper. Cook covered until rice is done.

Opossum Stew

Amounts	Ingredients
1	Opossum
water to cover to parboil	
1 ½ gallons	water
2 medium	onions, chopped
2 teaspoons	salt
2 cups	rice
2 pods	hot pepper, chopped

Directions

1. Clean and wash opossum. Cut up into pieces.
2. Boil opossum in salt water for 30 minutes in pot
   Over hot coals. Discard water.

3. Cover parboiled meat with water and add onion and salt. Cook covered for 45 minutes.
4. Stir in remaining ingredients and cook for 30 minutes
   Or until desired doneness.

Cabbage Stew

Amounts	Ingredients
2 gallons	water
1	chicken thighs, chopped
1 tablespoon	salt
1 cup	wild rice
1	onion, chopped
1	cabbage, chopped

Directions

1. Place water and chicken thighs in large pot and cook over heated coals until done.
2. Stir in rice and onion and cook for 30 minutes.
3. Stir in cabbage and cook for 20 minutes.

PRE AND POST REVIEWS

Former Maryland Slaves Informants

1. Mary Moriah page 34
    Anne Susanna Jones
    618 Raw Street
    Baltimore, Maryland

    Interviewed in Sept. 1937 by James O. Jones

    (Both parents were owned by Silas Thurston Randorph a distant relatives of Patrick Henry. She lived on the James River in Virginia.)

    "I was told that grandparents he got religion and prayed that God would set him free and grandma free."

    "I have seen slaves sold in the farm, and I have seen slaves brought to the farm. The slaves were brought to the farm. The slaves were brought up the river by boats and unloaded at the landing some crying and some seem to be happy."

2. Phillip Johnson
    Poolesville, Maryland
    Interviewed by Guthrie 9/14/1937; age 90 years born in Montgomery County.

3. George Jones
    At African M.E. Home
    Alsquith St. Baltimore
    Baltimore, Maryland
    Born in Frederick County
    84 years in 1863
    "Fireplace built to heat and cook food."

BIBLICAL SCRIPTURE

PSALM 107:19

19 Then they cry unto the Lord in their trouble, and to saveth them out of their distresses.

CHAPTER 19

ENTREES COURSE

Recipes That May Have been Used by the First African Slaves of Maryland
For Entrees or Meats:

ENTREES RECIPES

Roasted Rack of Goat

Amounts	Ingredients
1 -20 pounds	whole baby goat, cleaned and split into half.
2 cups	lard
1 cup	salt
½ cup	cracked black pepper
3 cups	Apple Cider Vinegar (for mopping)

Directions

1. Clean, split goat and rub down with lard.
2. In a bowl, mix together salt and black pepper
3. Rub mixture on outside and inside of goat. Set aside for 2 hours.
4. Build heating rack for goat. Make a grill using hot coals.
5. Place goat on rack and grill for 15 hours.
6. During cooking, use vinegar for mopping meat from time to time

Chicken and Dumplings

Amounts	Ingredients
1	hen, cut-up
1	onion, cut-up
2 teaspoons	salt
1 gallon	water

Dumplings	
3 cups	flour
1 teaspoon	salt
1 teaspoon	baking soda
1 cup	lard
1 cup	water, hot

Directions

1. Clean chicken, cut up and wash. Place chicken, salt, onion and water in a large black pot. Bring to a boil and cover. Cook over hot coals for 1 hour.
2. While chicken is cooking, make dumplings.
3. To make dumpling: stir together flour, salt, baking soda, and lard in a large bowl.
4. Stir in hot water. Make into large dough ball. Then pinch dough ball into 24 small-1/2 -inch balls.
5. Remove chicken from pot. Save liquid.
6. Cut up chicken and destroy bones. Place chicken back in broth.
7. While chicken is cooking, stir few dough balls at a time until all are the black pot and cook until done.
8. Cook until desired doneness.

Roasted Turkey

Amounts	Ingredients
1-20 pound	turkey, farm -raised
2 cups	salt
2 gallons	water
2 cups	onions, quartered
2 cups	butter

Directions

1. Clean and wash turkey. Destroy the pin feather.
2. Set turkey aside. In a large black pot, stir together salt and water.
3. Boil for 10 minutes. Add turkey and cover. Cook for 30 minutes.
4. Cool down and remove turkey. Destroy water.
5. Put onions in the cavity of turkey. Rub turkey on outside and inside with butter.
6. Place turkey in a large Dutch oven. Place over low coals and cook for 3 hours.
7. Test for doneness.

Fish Boil

Amounts	Ingredients
4 gallons	water
1 tablespoon	salt
2	red pepper pods, chopped
2 pounds	small red potatoes
2	onions, quartered
2 pounds	corn cobbetts
2 pounds	shrimp, deveined
3 pounds	crab legs

Directions

1. Dig a large pit in the ground, make a fire and place large black pot over fire.
2. Add water, salt, pepper pods, potatoes, onions and corn cobbetts and cook for 30 minutes.
3. Stir in shrimp and crab legs. Cook for ten minutes.

Maryland Ham-Fried

Amounts	Ingredients
1 -10 pounds	country-cured ham, sliced

Direction

1. Wash ham and slice.
2. Heat up skillet in fireplace.
3. Fry each slice of ham on both sides in the skillet until done.

Chicken Pot Pie

Amounts	Ingredients
1	fryer, cut up
1 quart	water
1 teaspoon	salt
2 cups	white potatoes, cubed
½ cup	onion, chopped
1 cup	whole kernel corn
2 cups	green peas
1 cup	carrots, cubed
For crust	
2 cups	flour
1 teaspoon	salt
½ cup	lard
¾ cup	water, cold

Directions for crust:

1. In a bowl, stir together flour and salt. Stir in lard.
2. Stir in water. Make into ball.

For Filling:

1. Boil chicken in a Dutch oven over hot coals until tender. Remove chicken
   From liquid, keep liquid, and chop chicken; destroy bones and skin.
2. Stir chopped chicken, potatoes, onion, corn, peas and carrots
3. Cook covered for 15 minutes.
4. Spread crust on top of the Dutch Oven. Make slits in top of crust.
5. Bake in Dutch oven for 1 hour.

Oxtails/Rice

Amounts	Ingredients
2 pounds	ox tails(cow tails) chopped
2 tablespoons	salt
2 gallons	water
1	onion, cubed
2cups	rice
1 teaspoon	black pepper

Directions

1. Clean and wash oxtails. Boil oxtails with salt in water for one hour in a big black pot over hot coals.
2. Add onion and rice. Stir. Cook covered.
3. Season with black pepper.
4. Cook until desired doneness.

PRE AND POST SLAVE REVIEWS

1. Alice Lewis
    Baltimore, Maryland
    Interviewed by Ellen B. Verfield on)May 18. 1937

    (84 years old; born in slavery; born in Wilkes County, GA; came to Baltimore-Wakefield Plantation live with I was 'leven and then given to a young mistress when she married and went to North Carolina to live; I seed these men and his sojers, gathering all the hogs and all of the hosses and cows.")

2. Perry Lewis
    1124 E. Lexington Street
    Baltimore, Maryland
    Interviewed by Rogers September 4, 1937

    (Born in Kent Island; father a freeman and mother a slave. The Eastern Shore of Maryland was in the most productive slave territory and where farming was done

    On a large scale and in that part of Maryland where there were many poor people.)

BIBLICAL SCRIPTURE

PSALM 107:20

20 He sent his word, and healed them, and delivered them from their destruction.

CHAPTER 20

STARCH ACCOMPANIMENTS

Recipes That May Have Been Used by the First
African Slaves of Maryland for Starch Accompaniments

Cornbread Dressing

Amounts	Ingredients
4 cups	chicken broth
2 cups	onions, chopped
4 cups	corn bread, crumbled
2 cups	biscuits, crumbled
2	eggs, whipped
1 teaspoon	salt
½ teaspoon	sage
1 teaspoon	black pepper

Directions

1. Make chicken broth by boiling necks, gizzards and Livers in a 2 gallons of water until done.
2. Keep broth. Chop meat, destroy bones and skin.
3. Stir chopped meat and remaining ingredients in Broth.
4. Pour mixture in a large Dutch oven and cover.
5. Bake for one hour or until done.

Jollof Rice

Amounts	Ingredients
3	onions, chopped
¼ cup	butter, melted
4 cups	rice, cooked
3 cups	broth
1 teaspoon	salt
1 teaspoon	black pepper

Directions

1. In a large skillet, cook onions in butter until tender.
2. Stir in rice, broth, salt and black pepper.
3. Cook for 10 minutes.

Corn Pudding

Amounts	Ingredients
5 cups	corn, scraped from cobs
½ cup	flour
¼ cup	onion, minced
½ cup	brown sugar
1	green pepper pod, minced
3 cups	milk
1 teaspoon	salt

Directions

1. Peel, wash and scrape corn cobs. Place in a bowl.
2. Whip all ingredients into corn.
3. Pour into a large Dutch oven and cook over coals for 45 minutes or until done.

PRE-AND POST REVIEWS

Former Maryland Informants Slaves

1. Richard Macks
   341 W. Biddle St.
   Baltimore, Maryland

Born in Charles County in Southern Maryland in 1844. Charles County, the county that James Wilkes Booth took refuge after the assassination of President Lincoln in 1865.

Bryantown

Near Bryantown, a county center prior to the Civil War as a market for tobacco, grain and market for slaves.

Bryantown, there was several storms, two or three taverns or inns which were well known in their day's for their hospitality to their guests to house slaves. There were both had long shed, strongly built with cells downstairs for men and a large room above for women at night the slave trade then charges to the owner, pay for their meals which were served on a long table in the shed, then afterwards, they were locked up for the night.

Colored Women Hard Times

"Let me explain to you very plain without prejudices one way or the other. I have had many opportunities a chance to watch white men and women, in my long career, colored women have many hard battles to fight to protect themselves from assault by employers, white male servants or by white men many times not being able to protect, in fear of losing their portions. Subjected then on the other hand there were many impositions by the women of the household."

2. Tom Randall
   Oella, Maryland

   Mollie was the cook at Howard House Born in Ellicott City,
   Howard County.
   Maryland in 1856.I remember
   When President.

BIBLICAL SCRIPTURE

PSALM 107:21

21 Oh that man would praise the Lord for his goodness, and for his
wonderful works to the children of men.

CHAPTER 21

VEGETABLE ACCOMPANIMENTS

Possible Recipes That May Have Been Used by the First African Slaves of Maryland

VEGETABLE ACCOMPANIMENTS.

Fried Eggplant

Amounts	Ingredients
2 cups	lard
4 cups	eggplant, sliced
4	eggs, beaten
2 cups	corn meal
1 teaspoon	salt

Directions

1. Heat lard to hot in a large black skillet.
2. Wash and slice eggplant. Beat eggs in a bowl.
3. In a bowl, stir together cornmeal and salt.
4. Dip each eggplant slice in the beaten eggs and then in corn meal.
5. Fry coated eggplant slices in hot lard.
6. Serve hot.

Mustard Greens/Hot Peppers

Amounts	Ingredients
1 quart	water
1	ham hock, cured
2 bunches	mustard greens
1 teaspoon	salt
2	hot pepper pods, chopped
3 tablespoons	lard
1 tablespoon	brown sugar

Directions

1. In a large black pot over hot coals, add water and ham hocks boil until ham hocks are tender.
2. Stir in greens, salt, hot pepper pods, lard and brown sugar Cover and cook for one hour.
3. Check for desired doneness.

Chow Chow

Amounts	Ingredients
1 head	cabbage, chopped
4 pods	hot green peppers, chopped
4 pods	hot red peppers, chopped
2 medium	onions, quartered
2 tablespoons	salt
1 gallon	apple cider vinegar

Directions

1. Grind all vegetables together. Place in a large pan. Add salt.
2. Stir well and add vinegar. Cook cover for one hour.
3. Stirring constantly.
4. Cook until desired doneness.

Boiled Collard Greens/Cured Meat

Amounts	Ingredients
1 gallon	water
¼ pound	cured meat, chopped
1 teaspoon	salt
¼ cup	sugar
2 bunches	collard greens, chopped
3	hot pepper pods, chopped
2 tablespoons	lard

Directions

1. Boil cured meat in water in a big black pot over coals.
2. Stir in collard greens and other ingredients.
3. Cover and cook for 1 ½ hours or until desired doneness.

Succotash

Amounts	Ingredients
1 gallon	water
1	ham hock, cured
1 pound	butter beans
½ pound	pinto beans
2 cups	carrots, chopped
2 cups	whole kernel corn

Directions

1. Boil ham hock in water until tender. Add butter beans and pinto beans.
2. Cover and cook for one hour.
3. Stir in carrots and whole kernel corn.
4. Cook for 30 minutes.

Boiled Kale Greens

Amounts	Ingredients
1 gallon	water
½ pound	meat cured, chopped
1 bunch	kale
1` teaspoon	salt
1 medium	onion, sliced
1 pod	red pepper, chopped

Directions

1. In a large black pot, boil meat in water until meat is done.
2. Stir in kale, salt, onion slices and red pepper.
3. Cook covered over hot coals until desired doneness.

Boiled Butter Beans

Amounts	Ingredients
1 gallon	water
½ pound	cured meats, chopped
½ pound	butter beans
1 teaspoon	salt
1 pod	red hot pepper, chopped

Directions

1. In a large black pot over hot coals, add water and cured meat, cover and cook until tender.
2. Stir in butter beans, salt and red hot pepper. Cover.
3. Cook for 45 minutes.

PRE-AND POST SLAVE REVIEWS

1. Dennis Simms
    425 Kosher Street
    Baltimore, Maryland

    Born on a tobacco plantation on June 17, 1841
    In Prince County.
    Type of bread, hominy, black strap molasses and a red herring
    a day and possum."
    He voted for President Lincoln and witness the second
    inauguration of Lincoln, after he was set free.

BIBLICAL SCRIPTURE

PSALM 107:22

22 And let them sacrifice the sacrifice of thanksgiving and declare his
works with rejoicing.

CHAPTER 22

BREADS AND BEVERAGES

Possible Recipes That May Have Been Used By First African Slaves of Maryland for Breads and Beverages

Egg Bread

Amounts	Ingredients

Cracklin' Bread

Amounts	Ingredients
1 cup	meat skins, chopped
2 cups	corn meal
½ cup	flour
1 teaspoon	baking soda
1 teaspoon	salt
1 cup	water
1	egg, beaten
1 cup	milk
2 tablespoons	lard

Directions

1. In a Dutch oven, cook meat skins until crispy. Set aside.
2. In a bowl, stir together corn meal, flour, baking soda and salt.
3. Add water, beaten egg, milk and lard. Stir well. Add crispy meat skins.
4. Pour batter into Dutch oven and cook over hot coals until done.
5. Cool and serve.

Hush Puppies

Amounts	Ingredients
2 cups	lard
2 cups	cornmeal
2 teaspoons	salt
½ cup	onion minced
1 cup	water

Directions

1. Heat lard to hot in a Dutch Oven over hot coals.
2. In the bowl, stir together corn meal salt, onion and water.
3. Make into balls, fry until crispy.
4. Drain and serve.

Spoon Bread

Amounts	Ingredients
4 cups	corn meal
1 cup	flour
1 teaspoon	soda
½ cup	lard
1 cup	buttermilk

Directions

1. In a bowl, mix together all ingredients.
2. Beat well.
3. Heat 2 tablespoons of lard in the bottom of a Dutch Oven.
4. Pour mixture in bottom of the hot Dutch oven.
5. Cover and bake over hot coals for 45 minutes.

Skillet Corn Bread

Amounts	Ingredients
2 cups	corn meal
1 cup	flour
1 teaspoon	salt
1 teaspoon	soda
1 cup	buttermilk
1 tablespoon	lard, soften

Directions

1. In a bowl, mix together corn meal, flour, salt and soda.
2. Stir in buttermilk and lard.
3. Place large black skillet up over hot coals. Heat 2 tablespoons lard up in bottom of large black skillet.
4. Pour corn meal mixture in bottom of skillet cook until done and then turn bread over so that bottom will become The top.

Ash Cakes

Amounts	Ingredients
3 cups	corn meal
2 ½ teaspoons	salt
1 cup	water
12	collard green leaves -use for wrapping cakes.

Directions

1. In a bowl, mix together all ingredients; except collard greens.
2. Roll ½ cup of mixture in each of the collard leaves.
3. Place in hot ashes and cook until done.

BEVERAGES

Peach Brandy

Amounts	Ingredients
4 gallons	soft peaches, mashed
2 gallons	hot water
2 pounds	sugar

Directions

1. Core peaches and chop up. Place in large crock container and set aside.
2. Heat together water and sugar until makes a light syrup.
3. Cool and pour over peaches. Place cheese cloth on top.
4. Place in a cool dry place for one week stir daily.
5. Strain and discard solids. Let age for 4 weeks.

PRE AND POST SLAVERY REVIEWS

1. Jim Taylor
   Baltimore, Maryland
   Born in Talbot County, Eastern Shore Maryland
   Born about 1847, age 90 years old. Parents owned by Mr. Davis of St. Micheals. Escaped to Chester and moved to around Philadelphia. Allen's Mission, a colored church that was used for escaping slaves in Philadelphia."

BIBLICAL SCRIPTURES

PSALM 107:23,24

23 They that go down to the sea, in ships that do business in great waters:

24 These see the works of the Lord, and his wonders in the deep.

CHAPTER 23

DESSERTS COURSE

Recipes That May Have Been Used by First African Slaves of Maryland for Desserts.

Desserts Recipes:

Egg Custard Pie

Amounts	Ingredients
For filling:	
1	eggs,
2	beaten
2 cups	brown sugar
1 cup	milk
½ teaspoon	grated nutmeg

Directions

1. In a bowl, beat eggs and gradually add sugar.
2. Beat until sugar is dissolved.
3. Stir in milk and nutmeg. Set aside.

For Crust:

1 ½ cups	flour
1 teaspoon	salt
¾ cup	lard
½ cup	water

Directions

1. In a bowl, stir together flour and salt.
2. Cut in lard.
3. Slowly stir in water.
4. Make into a ball and mash out in bottom of pan.
5. Pour filling over crust and place pan over medium hot ashes and cook covered for 30 minutes.

Peach Cobbler

Amounts	Ingredients
4 cups	peach slices
1 cup	water
1 ½ cups	brown sugar
½ cup	butter, soften
1 cup	milk
½ teaspoon	vanilla bean

Directions

1. Place all ingredients in a bowl and stir well.
2. Stir together ¼ cup water and 2 tablespoons flour.
3. Slowly add into peach mixture.
4. Cook over low coals in Dutch Oven in fireplace For 30 minutes. Cool place crust on top.

For Crust:

Crust

Amounts	Ingredients
2 cups	flour
1 teaspoon	salt
½ cup	lard
½ cup	water

Directions

1. In a bowl, stir in flour, salt and lard.
2. Stir in water.
3. Make into a ball. Using your hands, make into 8 -inch Circle.

For cobbler:

1. Place crust on top of peach mixtures. Make slits in crust.
2. Place top of Dutch Oven and cook for 45 minutes.

Berry Cobbler

Amounts	Ingredients
4 cups	black berries
2 cups	sugar
1 tablespoon	flour
1 cup	water
½ cup	butter, melted

Directions

1. Stir all ingredients and pour into a Dutch Oven.
2. Place crust on top of berry mixture.

For topping:

Amounts	Ingredients
2 cups	flour
1/2 cup	sugar
½ teaspoon	salt
1/3 cup	lard
1 cup	water

Directions

1. Stir together flour, sugar and salt.
2. Cut in lard. Stir in water.
3. Make into a 10 small balls. Flatten out each ball and place on top of berry mixture.
4. Cook in Dutch Oven covered. Cook over Low heat.

Sweet Potato Pudding

Amounts	Ingredients
4 cups	mashed sweet potatoes
1	eggs, beaten
1½ cups	brown sugar
½ cup	butter, soften
1 ½ cups	milk

Directions

1. Mix together all ingredients
2. Stir well. Place in a large pan and cook over low heat.

Sweet Potato Pie

Amounts	Ingredients
For filling	
3 cups	mashed sweet potatoes
1 ½ cups	brown sugar
1 cup	milk
½ cup	butter, melted
3 Eggs,	beaten

Directions

1. In a bowl, beat together all ingredients. Set aside.

For crust:

Amounts	Ingredients
1 ½ cups	flour
1 teaspoon	salt
½ cup	lard
¾ cup	water

Directions

1. Stir together flour and salt. Cut in lard.
2. Gradually add water.
3. Make a ball. Press ball out in a pan.
4. Prick the crust with a knife.
5. Pour sweet potato filling over crust. Cover.
6. Cook over hot coals until done.

Vinegar Pie

Amounts	Ingredients
5 cups	eggs, beaten
2 cups	sugar
2 cups	milk
¼ cup	vinegar

Directions

1. Whip together all ingredients and set aside.
2. Make crust.

Pie Crust

Amounts	Ingredients
2 cups	flour
2 tablespoons	brown sugar
1 teaspoon	salt
1 cup	butter
¾ cup	water

Directions

1. In a bowl, stir together flour, brown sugar and salt.
2. Cut butter into mixture.
3. Gradually add water and make into a ball.
4. Press ball into flat surface in the bottom of a pan.
5. Pour pie filling on top. Cover and cook over hot coals for 30 minutes or until done.

Pound Cake

Amounts	Ingredients
1 pound	butter, soften
3 cups	sugar
6	eggs
4 cups	flour
1 pint	milk

Directions

1. In a bowl, stir together butter and sugar.
2. Add eggs one at a time. Beat well after each addition.
3. Stir in flour ¼ cup at a time with ¼ cup milk.
4. Stir well. Continue until all ingredients are used.
5. Place in Dutch Oven and cover. Cook over hot coals

Jelly Cake

Amounts	Ingredients
3 cups	flour
1 teaspoon	salt
1 teaspoon	soda
1 ½ cups	butter
1 ½ cups	sugar
2	Eggs
1 ½ cups	grape Jelly for filling

Directions

1. Stir together flour, salt and soda. Set aside.
2. Cream together butter, sugar and eggs.
3. Beat in flour and egg mixture slowly.
4. Add milk and beat well.
5. Grease a 13 x 9 x2 baking pan. Pour mixture the long pan.
6. Bake over hot coals until done.
7. Cool and cut into half for top and bottom layer,
8. Spread grape jelly on top of bottom layer.
9. Place second layer on top of bottom layer.

PRE AND POST SLAVERY REVIEWS

1. James Wiggins
   825 Barre Street
   Baltimore, Maryland

   Born in Anne Arundell County. His father was bought at a auction sale held in Baltimore about 1845.

BIBLICAL SCRIPTURE

PSALM 100:3

2 Know ye the Lord he is God: it is he that hath made us, and not we ourselves: we are His people and the sheep of his pasture.

CHAPTER 24

SNACKS

Possible Recipes That May Have Been Used by the First African Slaves of Maryland For Snacks.

SNACKS RECIPES:

Cane Syrup Cookies

Amounts	Ingredients
2 cups	flour
1 teaspoon	salt
½ teaspoon	soda
1 ½ cups	butter
1 cup	cane syrup

Directions

1. Place flour, salt and soda in a bowl. Mix well. Set aside.
2. In a second bowl, stir butter and syrup together.
3. Stir together with flour mixture and roll into a large bowl.
4. Make into 20 small balls. Place each ball on a pan.
5. Flatten out and cook over hot coals until done.

Souse Meat

Amounts	Ingredients
1	hog's head, cleaned and eyes removed
2	pig's ears, cleaned
½ cup	salt
3 gallons	water
1	onions, quartered
4 pods	red hot peppers, chopped
1 gallon	vinegar

Directions

1. In a large black pot, place lean hog's head, pig's ears, salt Water, onion and red hot peppers.
2. Cook over hot coals for 1 ½ hours. Remove meat from water.
3. Chop meat very fine and discard bones.
4. Stir in vinegar and beat well. Press into two pans.
5. Set for 2 hours before servings.

Fried Pork Chop/Biscuit

Amounts	Ingredients
6	medium size pork chops
1 ½ teaspoons	black pepper
1 ½ teaspoons	salt
2 cups	flour
2 cups	lard

Directions

1. Wash each pork chop.
2. Season each chop with black pepper and salt.
3. Coat with flour.
4. Heat oil in large black skillet over hot coals.

5. Fry 3 chops at a time-10 minutes and turn and 5 minutes on second side.
6. Serve with biscuits.

Biscuits

Amounts	Ingredients
2 cups	flour
1 teaspoon	salt
1 teaspoon	soda
½ cup	lard
1 cup	buttermilk

Directions

1. In a bowl, stir together flour, salt and soda.
2. Stir in lard.
3. Stir in buttermilk. Make into biscuits.
4. Grease bottom of pan. Place biscuits in the pan. Cover.
5. Cook over hot coals.
6. Cook for 30 minutes. Remove from heat and make a sandwich.

Fried Pork Skins

Amounts	Ingredients
1	large skins, cut into 4" x 2" strips
1 gallon	lard
½ cup	salt

Directions

1. Prepare pig skins.
2. Heat lard in a large black pot.
3. Fry skins until puffed.
4. Remove from fat and sprinkle with salt.

Tea Cakes

Amounts	Ingredients
4 cups	flour
1 teaspoon	salt
1 teaspoon	soda
1 cup	sugar
½ cup	butter, soften
1 cup	milk

Directions

1. In a bowl, mix together flour, salt and soda. Set aside.
2. In a bowl, stir together sugar and butter.
3. Alternate stirring together sugar mixture and flour mixture with the milk.
4. Make tea cakes, by placing ½ cup of mixture 2 inches apart on a cooking pan.
5. Bake for 15 minutes or until done.

Pecan Pralines

Amounts	Ingredients
2 cups	brown sugar
½ teaspoon	salt
½ cup	butter
1 cup	cream
2 cups	pecan halves

Directions

1. In a large pan, mix together brown sugar, salt, butter and cream.
2. Bring to a boil, stir constantly until sugar is dissolved and mixture thickens.
3. Remove from heat and add pecan halves.
4. Place on plates in 2-inch round shapes. Cool and serve.

Peanut Brittle

Amounts	Ingredients
2 cups	sugar
½ cup	cane syrup
1 teaspoon	salt
4 cups	peanuts
1 teaspoon	soda
2	tablespoons butter for pan

Directions

1. In heavy black skillet, stir together sugar and cane syrup.
2. Stir constantly until sugar is melted about 15 minutes.
3. Stir in salt and peanuts. Cook for 10 minutes.
4. Stir in soda and pour over buttered pan.
5. Let cool and then break into pieces.

Fried Corn Pops

Amounts	Ingredients
1 cup	dried corn kernels
1 cup	lard
1 tablespoon	salt

Directions

1. Heat lard in skillet to hot.
2. Place dried corn kernels in skillet and cook for 10 minutes.
3. Cool and sprinkle salt over corn. Serve.

PRE AND POST SLAVERY REVIEWS

1. Rezin (Parson) William
   2010 Pierpoint Street
   Baltimore, Maryland

   Interview 18 and 24, 1937

   Oldest living Negro Civil War Veteran, now 110 oldest request in Maryland oldest freeman in American. He worked for George Washington. He worked for George Washington and attended President Lincoln's inauguration and Democratic

   Inaugurations.

   "President Lincoln, William says, was looked upon by many slaves as a messenger from heaven. Most slave owners was just drivers and the slaves were work horses for them."

REGION OF THE STATE

Tidewater Region is in the eastern part of the state. During slavery, the area produced corn, wheat, tobacco and slaves.

BIBLICAL SCRIPTURES

PSALM 100:4,5

2 Enter his gates with thanksgiving and into his courts with praise; be thankful to him and bless his name.

3 For the Lord is good, his mercy is everlasting; and his truth endureth to all generations.

PART III

MASSACHUSETTS

CHAPTER 25

The First Thanksgiving Celebration was said to be an effort between the Pilgrims and Wampanoag Indians in Massachusetts in 1621. The activity took place in the harvest season, the autumn season. The menu included turkey, dressing, vegetables and pumpkin pie. The Wampanoag Indians supplied vegetables such as green beans, lettuce, spinach, cabbage, carrots and peas.

The slaves were just arriving on slave ships to the colony, they had to make cooking utensils made from trees, such as, plates, bowls, spoons, forks, and stirring utensils. Iron skillets and black pots were, sometimes, brought from Africa. The plantation owners had given limited cooking procedures to the slaves and the slaves had to cook outside.

The purpose of this chapter is to illustrate how the slaves may have done their cooking, menus that may have been selected, recipes for the foods, pre-and post slavery reviews containing information about former Massachusetts' slaves and other former slaves and biblical scriptures. In the pre and post slavery reviews the time span of extend from the 1600s up through the 1900s.

I. Possible Food Sources Available to the First African Slaves of Massachusetts for Thanksgiving and Christmas.

Foods	Sources
1. Meats: fish, poultry, fish, pork, wild life	Slave owners, Atlantic Ocean, and rivers, Plantations
2. Vegetables	Wampanoag Indians-green beans, onions, corn
3. Fruits	wild fruit
4. Breads and cereals Flour, rice	Indian corn slave ships
5. Milk and dairy	plantation owners
6. Seasonings, sugar, molasses spices	slave ships and slaves
7. Coffee, peanuts	Africa
8. Salt	Atlantic Ocean
9. Honey	Indians
10. Water	Spring water, Indians

Cooking Utensils may have been developed from wood from trees, rocks and iron. The Africans were said to have brought iron pots with them.

ABOUT MASSACHUSETTS

MASSACHUSETTS
(SLAVE STATE -1788-1865? Some Slaves were freed
Before the Civil War.)
(MA)

BAY STATE, OLD COLONY

CAPITOL: Boston

HISTORY: The Pilgrims, seeking freedom, made their first settlement at Plymouth, 1620; the following year they gave thanks to their survival with the first Thanksgiving Day. Indian opposition reached a high point in King Philip's 1675-76, won by the colonists. Demonstrations against British restrictions set off the "Boston Massacre" 1770, and Boston 'Tea Party', 1773. First bloodshed of the Revolution was set at Lexington 1775.

STATE
DATA:

Motto:	Ense Petit Placidam Sub Libertate Quietam (By the sword we seek peace, but peace only under liberty)	
Flower:	Mayflower	
Bird:	Chickadee	
Tree:	American elm.	
Song:	All Hail to Massachusetts	
Entered union:	Sixth of the original 13 states to ratify Constitution, February 6, 1778	
People:	Racial distribution; White(major ethnic groups Canadian, Italian, Irish, English, Polish), Blacks, Hispanics	

Geography:	Total area.8,257 square miles, Rank: 45 Land area.7,826 square miles; Acres forested
Land:	2,952,300
Location:	New England State along Atlantic seaboard.
Climate:	Temperature with colder and drier climate in Western region.
Topography:	Jagged indented coast from Rhode Island Around Cape Cod; flat land yields to stony Upland pastures near central region and Gentle hilly country in west, except in west, land is Rocky, and not fertile.
ECONOMY:	Principal industries: manufacturing, services, trade, construction
Principal manufactured goods:	Electronics, machinery, instruments,
	Fabricated metals, printing and publishing.
Agriculture:	Chief crops, nursey, green house, products, miscellaneous vegetables, apples, tobacco, corn, potatoes
Livestock:	Cattle, hogs/pigs, sheep, horses, ponies, poultry
Timber/Lumber:	white pine, oak, other hardwoods.
Minerals:	Sand and gravel, stone
Chief ports:	Boston, Fall River, Salem, Gloucester

Major international airport at:	Boston
Tourist attractions:	Cape Cod with Provincetown Artists' Colony; Berkshire Music Festival, Tanglewood, Boston "Pop" concerts: Museum of Fine Arts, Arnold Arboretum, both Boston, Jacob's Pillow Dance Festival, West Becket, historical Shaker Village Old Sturbridge, Lexington, Concord, Salem, Plymouth Rock
School:	In 1636, Harvard University was founded. Harvard is the oldest college in the United States.
FAMOUS "BAY STATERS":	Include Samuel Adams. Louisa May Alcott, Horatio Alger, Clara Barton, Emily Dickinson, Emerson, Hancock, Hawthrone, Oliver W. Holmes, Winslow Homer, Eliza Howe, Samuel F.B. Morse, Poe, Revere; Sargent, Thoreau, Whistler, Whittier Francis Scott Key-Author of the National Anthem and Fought for the freedom of slaves.

Sixteen travel regions will be included.

MASSACHUSETTS BAY COLONY WAS THE FIRST NEW ENGLAND COLONY TO BEGIN THE SLAVE INDUSTRY.

The Governor of Massachusetts, a slave owner, help to write the law legalizing slavery in North America.

PRE- AND POST SLAVERY REVIEWS

Massachusetts became the first slave holding New England Colony. The first slaves were reported to be in 1624 with 2 slaves belonging to a private slave owner.

BIBLICAL SCRIPTURE

PSALM 136:1

O Give thanks unto the Lord, for he is good, for his mercy endureth for ever;

CHAPTER 26

THANKSGIVING AND SNACKS MENUS

I. Two Possible Thanksgiving and Snack Menus That May Have Been
    Choices of First African Slaves of Massachusetts

Thanksgiving Menu:

I

Fried   Sausage Links
Stewed Crab Legs

Red Beans /Rice

Boiled Wild Turkey

Roasted Guinea Hens

Rice Dressing
Fried Potatoes

Boiled Green Beans
Baked Kidney Beans

Corn Pones
Sorghum Pie
Indian Pudding

Ginger Tea
Snacks
Boiled peanuts
Pickled Eggs

Thanksgiving Menu:

II

Pot Liquor
Smoked Herrings

Spinach Soup
Fish Head Soup
Smoked Venison Rump Roast
Fried Trout

Fried Grits
Carrots Soufflé
Sweet Potato Souffle

Buttermilk Biscuits
Cornmeal Biscuits
Ginger Bread
Raisin Pie
Coconut Cake

Snacks
Dried Peach Halves
Hoop Cheese Slices

PRE AND POST SLAVERY REVIEWS

The first African Slaves were imported directly from Africa to Massachusetts in 1634.

MASSACHUSETTS TRAVEL REGION

1. Greater Boston Region

BIBLICAL SCRIPTURE

PSALM 136:2

O give thanks unto God of gods: for his mercy endureth for ever.

CHAPTER 27

CHRISTMAS AND SNACKS MENUS

1. Two Possible Christmas and Snack Menus That May Have Been Chosen by the First African Slaves of Massachusetts.

I

Christmas Menu:
Liver Cheese Slices
Flapjacks/Maple Syrup

Squash Soup
Rabbit Meat Stew
Smoked Picnic Barbeque
Smoked Fish
Fried Potato Wedges
Wild Rice Stuffing
Rutabagus Greens
Boiled Okra Pods

Fried Peach Pies
Persimmons Pudding

Eggnog

Snacks
Fried Meat Skins
Sugar   Cane Joints

Christmas Menu:

II

Hoppin' Johns
Molasses Bread and Butter

Pumpkin and Goat Meat Stew
Green Split Pea Soup

Baked Raccoon and Sweet Potatoes

Fried Turkey

Oyster and Rice Dressing
Hominy Grits Casserole
Smothered   Wild Onions
Steamed Wild Asparagus

Cornbread Pones
Scones

Mincemeat Pie
Grits Pudding

Wild Grape Wine

Snacks

Fried Peanuts
Green Apples Slices

PRE AND POST SLAVERY PREVIEWS

Slave owners traded a ship load of African slaves in Boston in 1638. These slaves were bought from Barbados to Boston in exchange for a group of Pequot Indians, who were taken to Barbados.

MASSACHUSETTS TRAVEL REGION

2. North of Boston

BIBLICAL SCRIPTURE

PSALM 136:3

O Give thanks to the Lord of gods, for his mercy endureth forever

CHAPTER 28

APPETIZERS COURSES

Part I. Possible Recipes that May Have Been Used by First African Slaves from Massachusetts

FOR APPETIZERS.

Stewed Crab Legs

Amounts	Ingredients
2 pounds	crab legs
2 gallons	water
2 tablespoons	salt
2 medium	onions, quartered
1 leaf	sage

Directions

1. Clean crab legs while water is heating in a large black pot over hot coals.
2. Stir in salt and onions and sage.
3. Place crabs in black pots. Cook covered for 30 minutes.
4. Remove crab legs and drain. Serve with soft butter.

Fried Sausage Links

Amounts	Ingredients
1 pound	stuffed sausage links, pre made
1 tablespoon	lard

Directions

1. Use:
    Premade Stuffed sausage links: ground 2 pound lean sausage meat, 1 teaspoon cracked black pepper, 1 teaspoon salt, 2 sage leaves and 2 red pepper pods, dried.
    Stuff grounded meat in 1 =12 inch cleaned chitterling link.
    Let dry for 2 weeks.
2. Divide the sausage into 6- 2-inch pieces.
3. Heat lard in black skillet.
4. Fry meat for 15 minutes. Drain.
5. Serve with hot biscuits.

Hoppin' Johns

Amounts	Ingredients
1 cup	dried black eyed peas
1	red pepper pod, chopped
4 cups	water
1	ham hocks
1 ½ teaspoons	salt
2 cups	white rice, cooked

Directions

1. In a medium sized black pot, cook black-eyed peas, red pepper
    And water until black eyed peas are done.
2. Season with salt.
3. Serve over cooked rice.

Molasses Bread and Butter

Amounts	Ingredients
8	buttermilk biscuits
½ cup	molasses
½ cup	butter, pats

Directions

1. Prepare buttermilk biscuits, according to recipe.
2. Open biscuits and place on a pan.
3. Place 1 tablespoon of molasses and heat up.
4. Remove from heat and place one pat of butter on each biscuits.
5. Serve.

To make biscuits:

Buttermilk Biscuits

Amounts	Ingredients
2 cups	flour
1 tablespoon	soda
1 teaspoon	salt
½ cup	lard
1 ½ cups	buttermilk

Directions

1. Sift together flour, soda and salt in a bowl.
2. Stir in lard.
3. Stir in buttermilk.
4. Make into 2-inch biscuits, place in a Dutch oven cooking over hot coals and bake on high heat or until golden brown.

Pot Liquor

Amounts	Ingredients
2 cups	juice left over from cooked
Collard greens	
1 ½ cups	corn bread

Directions

1. Pour collard green juice in a heavy pot.
2. Stir in corn bread.
3. Stir until corn bread is dissolved.
4. Serve hot.

Smoked Herrings

Amounts	Ingredients
2 pounds	small herring fish
1 tablespoon	salt

Directions

1. Prepare a small grill by stretching chicken wire between two large rocks and heated hot coats.
2. Wash, salt and place fish on chicken wire and smoke on both sides for 10 minutes on each side.
3. Cool hot fish before service.

Liver Cheese Slices

Amounts	Ingredients
1 pound	beef liver, cleaned and membranes removed
1 ½ gallons	water
2 medium	onions, quartered
2 teaspoons	salt
½ cup	vinegar

Directions

1. Clean and wash beef liver. Cut into chunks.
2. Boil in water with onions and salt until done.
3. Drain and grind up.
4. Pour vinegar in mixture.
5. Make into large loaf. Store for 1 week.
6. Slice when serving.

Flapjacks/Maple Syrup

Amounts	Ingredients
2 cups	flour
1 teaspoon	salt
1 teaspoon	soda
2 tablespoons	sugar
1	egg, beaten
2 cups	milk
½ cup	lard
½ cup	maple syrup
2 tablespoons	butter

Directions

1. In a bowl, stir together flour, salt, soda and sugar.
2. Beat in egg and milk. Whip well.
3. Heat lard in a big skillet over hot coals.
4. Fry about 1/3 cup of batter at a time over heat.
5. Fry on both sides.
6. Serve hot with maple syrup and butter.

PRE-AND POST SLAVERY REVIEWS

Massachusetts has said to become among
the first states to abolish slavery.

MASSACHUSETTS TRAVEL REGION

4.   Greater Merrimack Valley

BIBLICAL SCRIPTURE

PSALM 136: 4

To him who alone doeth great wonders for his mercy endureth forever.

CHAPTER 29

SOUP AND STEW COURSES

I. Possible Recipes that May Have been Used By the First African Slaves of Massachusetts for Soups and Stews.

Red Beans/ Rice Soup

Amounts	Ingredients
1 cup	red beans, dried
6 cups	water
1	ham hock, cured
1	onion, chopped
1 teaspoon	salt
1 ½ teaspoons	sugar
1 cup	rice

Directions

1. Pick and wash beans. Place in a large black pot with water, ham hock and onion. Cover and cook over hot coals for 1 hour. Stir.
2. Add salt, sugar and rice.
3. Cook until rice is tender.
4. Serve.

Fish Head Soup

Amounts	Ingredients
1 pound	whiting fish heads
1 ½ gallons	water
½ pound	salt pork, cubed
1	onion, quartered
2 teaspoons	salt
1 cup	black-eyed peas
1 cup	rice

Directions

1. Clean and wash fish heads.
2. Place all other ingredients, except rice in a black pot Heated over hot coals.
3. Cook for 30 minutes. Stir in rice.
4. Cover and cook for 15 minutes. Test for doneness.

Crab Legs Soup

Amounts	Ingredients
1 gallon	water
¼ pound	salt pork, cubed
1 medium	onion, minced
1 pound	carrots, chopped
2 teaspoons	salt
½ pound	crab legs meat

Directions

1. Place water, salt pork and onion in large black pot and heat over hot coals and cover. Boil for 45 minutes.
2. Stir in remaining ingredients and cook for 30 minutes.
3. Serve.

Spinach Soup

Amounts	Ingredients
½ gallon	water
2 strips	salt pork, cubed
1 bunch	spinach
1 teaspoon	salt
1 medium	onion, minced

Directions

1. Boil water and salt pork together in a medium size pot Over hot coals until meat is tender.
2. Stir in remaining ingredients.
3. Cook 30 minutes or until desired doness.

Squash Soup

Amounts	Ingredients
½ gallon	water
2 strips	bacon, minced
1	onion, minced
3 cups	yellow squash, chopped
1 teaspoon	salt
2 tablespoons	brown sugar

Directions

1. In a big black pot, add water bacon and onion.
2. Boil over high heat until onion is tender.
3. Stir in squash, salt and brown sugar.
4. Cook for 30 minutes.

Rabbit Meat Soup

Amounts	Ingredients
1 gallon	water
1	rabbit, cleaned, washed and cut -up into pieces
2	pods, red pepper, chopped
3	carrots, chopped
2 medium	onions, chopped
2 tablespoons	salt
1 cup	rice

Directions

1. In a medium size black pot, add water, rabbit, red pepper, carrots and onions.
2. Cover and cook over hot coals for 30 minutes.
3. Test for doneness. Stir in salt and rice.

Pumpkin and Goat Meat Stew

Amounts	Ingredients
1 gallon	water
1 pound	goat meat chunks
1 strip	bacon, chopped
1	onion, chopped
2	hot green pepper, chopped
1 tablespoon	salt
¼ cup	brown sugar
2 cups	pumpkin, chopped

Directions

1. In a large black pot, place water, goat meat chunks, bacon, and Green pepper pods. Cover. Cook over hot coals for 45 minutes.

2. Stir in salt, brown sugar and pumpkin. Cook for 30 minutes.
3. Serve.

Green Split Pea Soup

Amounts	Ingredients
1 gallon	water
2 cups	dried green peas
1	ham hocks, cured
1 medium	onion, chopped
1 teaspoon	salt
2 pods	red pepper, chopped

Directions

1. Place water, dried green peas, ham hocks and onion in
   A large black pot. Stir well. Cover and cook over hot coals for
   1 hour.
2. Stir in salt and red peppers. Cover and cook for 1 hour.

PRE AND POST SLAVERY REVIEWS

In 1638, a ship named Desire brought African slaves from West Indies to Massachusetts. The slaves were brought in to help develop the state of Massachusetts.

MASSACHUSETTS TRAVEL REGION

3. Bristol County

BIBLICAL SCRIPTURE

PSALM 136: 26

26 O give thanks unto God of Heaven for mercy endureth for ever.

CHAPTER 30

ENTRÉE OR MEAT COURSES

Part I. Possible Recipes That May Have Been Used by First African Slaves of Massachusetts for Entrees.

Boiled Wild Turkey

Amounts	Ingredients
1	turkey
2 medium	onions, chopped
2 gallons	water
2 tablespoons	salt

Directions

1. Remove feathers, clean, gut and wash turkey.
2. Place whole turkey, onions, water and salt in a Large pot. Bring to a boil. Cover.

3. Boil over medium heat for 2 ½ hours.
4. Remove from pot. Slice and serve.

Roasted Guinea Hens

Amounts	Ingredients
6	guinea hens
½ cup	lard
2 tablespoons	salt

Directions

1. Remove feathers, clean and wash guinea hens. Boil in salty water until tender.
2. Drain and pat dry. Rub each hen with lard and salt.
3. Place each hen breast side down in Dutch oven and cover. Roast over hot coals for 30 minutes. Turn and continue cooking for 10 minutes.

Smoked Venison Rump Roast

Amounts	Ingredients
5 pounds	venison roast
½ cup	salt
¼ cup	black pepper, cracked

Directions

1. Make a 4 x 4 pit in the ground. Build a fire with coals.
2. Stretch a wire over heat.
3. Rub roast with salt and black pepper.
4. Place seasoned meat over heat and smoke slowly
   For 2 hours.

Fried Trout

Amounts	Ingredients
2 pounds	whole trout, cleaned and halved
2 tablespoons	salt
1 pound	yellow, cornmeal
1 pound	lard

Directions

1. Clean and cut fish in half.
2. Season with salt. Roll in corn meal.
3. Heat lard in large skillet over hot coals.
4. Fry each piece of fish until golden brown.

Smoked Picnic Ham Barbecue

Amounts	Ingredients
1	pork shoulder
2 teaspoons	salt
2 gallons	water

Directions

1. Clean and remove extra fat from shoulder. This becomes The first part of a picnic ham.
2. Rub with salt.
3. Place meat in water and cook for 2 hours.
4. Remove from water and drain.
5. Place over meat smoker built over hot coals.
6. Cook slowly for 14 hours.

Smoked Grouper Fish

Amounts	Ingredients
2 pounds	grouper fish
2 teaspoons	salt

Directions

1. Clean, wash and split fish in half.
2. Season with salt.
3. Smoke fish over hot coals in a pit.
4. Smoke 30 minutes on each side.

Baked Raccoon and Sweet Potatoes

Amounts	Ingredients
1	raccoon
2 tablespoons	salt
1	onion quartered
2 gallons	water
½ cup	lard
6 medium sized	sweet potatoes, sliced

Directions

1. Clean, remove internal organs and wash raccoon.
2. Split in half. Place in big black pot with salt, onion and water.
3. Cover and boil for 30 minutes.
4. Discard water. Place raccoon on a pan and rub with lard Place sweet potatoes around raccoon. Cover and cook for 1 ½ Hours or until desired doneness.

Fried Turkey

Amounts	Ingredients
1	turkey
2 teaspoon	salt
2 gallons	water
1 gallon	lard

Directions

1. Clean, remove internal organs and wash.
2. Place turkey, salt and water in large black pot. Cover.
3. Boil in water until tender. Remove from water. Discard water.
4. Pat turkey dry.
5. Clean large black pot and heat lard to hot. Fry whole turkey until golden brown.

PRE- AND POST SLAVERY REVIEWS

First Slaves for Puritans in Massachusetts

-The Puritans took slaves from Africa to Boston in slave ships that had begun in Madagascar.

MASSACHUSETTS TRAVEL REGION

5. Plymouth County

BIBLICAL SCRIPTURE

PSALM 140:1

Deliver me, O Lord from the evil man: preserve me from the violent man.

CHAPTER 31

STARCH ACCOMPANIMENTS

1. Possible Recipes That May Have Been Used by the First African Slaves of Massachusetts for Starch Accompaniments.

Rice Dressing

Amounts	Ingredients
4 cups	rice, cooked
2 medium	onions, minced
1 clove	garlic, minced
1 teaspoon	salt
1 teaspoon	black pepper
2 cups	turkey broth
1 cup	cooked turkey meat from neck
1 cup	gizzard and liver meat cooked, chopped

Directions

1. Stir all ingredients together. Pack in large pan and cook over low heat.

Fried Potatoes

Amounts	Ingredients
1 pound	white potatoes, quartered
4 cups	lard
2 teaspoons	salt
1 medium	onion, sliced

Directions

1. Peel and wash potatoes. Pat dry.
2. Heat lard in skillet over hot coals.
3. Cook potatoes for 5 minutes; stir in
   Salt and onion.
4. Cook for 30 minutes.

Fried Grits

Amounts	Ingredients
1 pound	cooked grits
Made into 8 patties	
1	Eggs, beaten
1 cup	flour
1 cup	lard

Directions

1. To make grits into patties: cook a recipe of grits and cool. Make cold grits into 8 patties.
2. Dip into egg mixtures and then coat with flour.
3. Heat lard until hot and then fry until golden brown.

Fried Sweet Potato Wedges

Amounts	Ingredients
6	sweet potatoes, slices
1 teaspoon	salt
1 cup	butter
½ cup	brown sugar

Directions

1. Wash and slice sweet potatoes. Season with salt.
2. Heat butter up in skillet. Fry sweet potatoes until tender.

3. Stir in brown sugar. Cover and cook for 15 minutes.
4. Stir. Serve.

Wild Rice Dressing

Amounts	Ingredients
2 cups	wild rice
4 cups	water
1 tablespoon	salt
1 teaspoon	black pepper
1 tablespoon	lard
1	onion, chopped
2	cloves garlic, minced

Directions

1. Cook rice in water and salt until tender.
2. Add remaining ingredients and cook until done.

Oysters and Rice Dressing

Amounts	Ingredients
2 medium	onions, minced
2 slices	bacon, chopped
2 cups	oysters, shucked
4 cups	rice, cooked
3 cups	chicken or turkey broth
1 teaspoon	salt
1 teaspoon	black pepper

Directions

1. In a large black pot, cook onions and bacon together for 2 -3 minutes.
2. Stir in oysters. Cook for 2 minutes.
3. Add rice and broth. Add black pepper and salt.

Hominy Grits Casserole

Amounts	Ingredients
4 cups	grits, cooked
1	onion, diced
2	eggs, beaten
2 cups	asparagus, cooked
3	hot pepper pods, chopped
½ cup	butter
1 cup	hoop cheese, grated
1 teaspoon	salt

Directions

1. Stir all ingredients together.
2. Pour into a Dutch oven and cook for 30 minutes.

PRE AND POST SLAVE REVIEWS

Africans, slaves and former slaves have been documented as inventors in United States.

	Name	Invention	Date Patent Granted
1.	Abrams, W.B	Home Attachment	April 14, 1891
2.	Allen, C.W.	Self-Leveling Table	Nov. 1, 1898
3.	Allen, J.B.	Clothes Line Support	Dec. 10,1895
4.	Asbourne, A.P.	Process for Preparing Coconut for Domestic Use	June 1.1875
5.	Ashbourne, A.P.	Biscuit Cutter	Nov. 30, 1875
6.	Ashbourne, A.P.	Refining Coconut G1	July 27, 1880
7.	Ashbourne, A.P.	Processing of Treating Coconut	August 21, 1877

8.	Bailes, W.A.	Ladder Scaffold Support	8-5-1879
9.	Bailey, LC	Combined Truss and Bandage	Sept. 25. 1883
10.	Bailey, L.C.	Folding Bed	July 18, 1899
11.	Bailiff, B.D.	Shampoo Headrest	Oct.11, 1898
12.	Ballow, W.J.	Combined Hatrol and Table	March 29, 1898
13.	Barnes, G.W.E.	Design for Sign	August 19, 1898
14.	Beard, A.J.	Rotary Engine	July 5, 1892
15.	Beard, A.J.	Car Coupler	Nov. 23, 1897
16.	Becket, G.E.	Letter Box	October 4, 1892
17.	Bell, L	Locomotive Smoke Stack	March 23, 1871
18.	Bell, L	Dough Kneader	Dec. 10, 1872
19.	Benjamin, L.W.	Broom Moisteners and Bridles	May 16, 1893
20.	Benjamin, Miss M.E.	Gong and Signal Chairs for Hotels	July 17, 1888
21.	Binga, M.W.	Street Sprinkling Apparatus	July 22,1879
22.	Blackburn,	Railway Signal	Jan10,1888
23.	Blackburn, A.B.	Cash Carrier	Oct. 23, 1888
24.	Blair, Henry	Corn Planter	Oct. 14, 1834
25.	Blair, Henry	Cotton Planter	Oct. 31, 1836
26.	Blue, L.	Hand Corn-Shelling Device	May 20, 1884
27.	Broker, L.F.	Design Rubber Scrape-Knife	March 28, 1899
28.	Boone, Sarah	Ironing Board	April 26, 1892
29.	Bowman, H.A.	Making Flags	Feb 23, 1892

30.	Brooks, C.B.	Punch	October 31, 1893
31.	Brooks, C.B.	Street Sweepers	March 17, 1896
32.	Brooks,	Halstead and Page Street Sweepers	April 12, 1896
33.	Brown, Henry	Receptors for Strong And Restoring Paper	Nov 2, 1886
34.	Brown, L.F.	Bridle Bit	Oct.25, 1892
35.	Brown, O.E.	Horse Show	August 23, 1892
36.	Brown and Latimer	Water Closets for Railway Cars	2/10/1874
37.	Burr, J.A.	Lawn Mower	May 9, 1899
38.	Burr, W.F.	Switching Devise for Railways	Oct. 31, 1899
39.	Burwell, W.	Boot or Shoe	November 28, 1888
40.	Butler, R.A.	Train Alarm	June 15, 1897
41.	Butts, J.W.	Luggage Carrier	Oct.10, 1899
42.	Byrd, T.J.	Apparatus for Detaching Horses from Carriages	March 19, 1872
43.	Byrd, T.T.	Improvement in Neck Yolks for Wagons	April 30, 1872
44.	Byrd, T.T.	Improvement in Car Coupling	Dec. 1, 1874
45.	Campbell, W.C.	Self-Setting Animal Trap	August 30, 1899
46.	Cargill, B.F,	Invalid Cot	July 25, 1888
47.	Carrington, J.A.	Range	July 25, 1888
48.	Carter, W.C.	Umbrella Stand	8-4-1885
49.	Certain, J.M.	Parcel Carrier for Bicycles	Dec 26, 1899

50.	Cherry, M.A.	Velocipede	May 8, 1888
51.	Cherry, M.A.	Street Car Fender	Jani, 1895
52.	Church, T.S.	Carpet Beating Machine	July 27, 1884
53.	Clare, O.B.	Trestle	Oct 9, 1888
54.	Coates, R	Overboot for Horses	4/19/1892
55.	Cook, G.	Automatic Fishing Device	May 30, 1899
56.	Coolidge, J.S.	Harness Attachment	Nov.13, 1888
57.	Cooper, A.R.	Shoemaker's Jack	8-22-1899
58.	Cooper, J.	Shutter and Fastening	May 1, 1883
59.	Cooper, J.	Elevator Devise	April 22, 1895
60.	Cooper, J.	Elevator Devise	Sept.21, 1893
61.	Cornwell, P.W.	Draft Regulator	Oct. 2, 1888
62.	Cornwell, R.W.	Draft Regulator	Feb. 7, 1893
63.	Cralle, A.L.	Ice Cream Mold	Feb.2. 1897
64.	Creamer, H	Steam Trap Feeder	March 17, 1895
65.	Creamer, H.	Steam Trap Feeder	Dec. 11, 1888
66.	Cosgrove, W.F.	Automatic Stop Plug For Gas Oil Pipes	Mar. 17, 1885
67.	Darkins, J. T.	Ventilations Aid	Feb 19,1895
68.	Davis, I.D.	Tonic	Nov. 2,1886
69.	Davis, I.D.	Riding Saddle	Oct. 6, 1886
70.	Davis, W.R. Jr	Library Table	Sept. 24, 1872
71.	Dietz, W.A.	Shoe	April 30, 1867
72.	Dickerson, J.H.	Planata Detroit Mech.	March 1899
73.	Dorticus, C.I.	Device for Applying Coloring Liquid to Side of Sole, Heels of Shoes	March 19, 1895
74.	Dortius, C.J.	Machine for Embossing Photo	April 16, 1895
75.	Dorticus, C.J.	Photographs Print Wash	April 23, 1895

76.	Dorticus, C.J.	Hose Leak Stop	JULY 18, 1899
77.	Downing, P.B.	Electric Switch for Railroads	June 17, 1890
78.	Downing, P.B.	Letter Box	Oct. 17, 1891
79.	Downing, P.B.	Street Letter Box	Oct. 17, 1891
80.	Dunning, J.H.	Horse Detacher	Mar. 17, 1897
81.	Edmonds, J.H.	Separating Screens	July 20, 1897
82.	Elkins, T.	Dining, Ironing Table and Quilting Frame Combined	Feb 22, 1870
83.	Elkins, T.	Chamber Commode	Jan. 9, 1892
84.	Elkins, T.	Refrigerator Apparatus	Nov. 4, 1879
85.	Evans, J.H.	Convertible Setters	October 5, 1897
86.	Faulkner, J.H.	Ventilated Shoe	April 29, 1870
87.	Ferrell, F. J.	Steam Trap	Feb. 11, 1890
88.	Ferrell, F.J.	Apparatus for Milking	May 27, 1890
89.	Fisher, D.A.	Furniture Caster	March 14, 1896
90.	Flemiming, R.F.	Guitar	Mar 3, 1886
91.	Goode, Sarah E.	Folding Cabinet Bed Bed	July 14, 1885
92.	Grant, G.F.	Golf-Tee	December 12, 1889
93.	Grant, W.S.	Curtain Rod Support	Aug.4, 1896
94.	Gray, R.H.	Baling Press	August 28, 1874
95.	Gray, R.H.	Cistern Cleaners	April 9, 1875
96.	Gray, R.H.	Baling Press	August 28, 1874
97.	Gregory, J.	Motor	April 26, 1887
98.	Grenon, H.	Razor Stropping Devise	Feb 18, 1896

| 99. | Griffin, F.W. | Pool Table Attachment | June 13, 1899 |
| 100. | Gunn, S.W. | Boot or Shoe | Jan.16, 1900 |

MASSACHUSETTS TRAVEL REGIONS

Martha's Vineyard

7.   Nantucket Island

BIBLICAL SCRIPTURE

PSALM 140:13

Surely the righteous shall give thanks unto thy name: the upright shall dwell in thy presence.

CHAPTER 32

VEGETABLE ACCOMPANIMENTS

Part I. Possible Recipes That May Have Been Used by the First African Slaves of Massachusetts for Vegetable Accompaniments.

I Boiled Green Beans

Amounts	Ingredients
2 cups	water
1	ham hock, cured
1 pound	green beans, snapped
1 teaspoon	salt

Directions

1. In a large black pot, boil water and ham hock until done.
2. Add green beans and stir in salt. Cover. Boil for 10 minutes.

Baked Kidney Beans

Amounts	Ingredients
2 cups	kidney beans, dried
4 cups	water
½ cup	onion, minced
1 cup	molasses
1 teaspoon	salt
½ cup	brown sugar
½ cup	hot water

Directions

1. In a large black pot, boil kidney beans in water until done.
2. Drain. Place kidney beans in a pan and stir in remaining ingredients.
3. Bake for 30 minutes.

Carrot Souffles

Amounts	Ingredients
2 cups	carrots, cooked
½ cup	brown sugar
1 teaspoon	salt
1 cup	milk
2	eggs, beaten
½ cup	butter, soften

Directions

1. In a bowl, mix all ingredients together.
2. Place in a pan and bake over low coals for 30 minutes.
3. Serve

Sweet Potato Soufflé

Amounts	Ingredients
4 cups	sweet potatoes, mashed
3	eggs, beaten
2 cups	cream
½ cup	butter, soften
½ cup	brown sugar
1 teaspoon	salt
2 tablespoons	flour

Directions

1. Stir together all ingredients.
2. Place in a large pan and cook for 45 minutes.

Boiled Rutabagas Greens

Amounts	Ingredients
2 cups	water
2 strips	country cured meat
2 bunches	rutabagas greens, chopped
1 teaspoon	salt
2 tablespoons	sugar
1 pod	hot pepper, chopped
2 tablespoons	lard

Directions

1. Using a large black pot, boil water and country cured meat for 30 minutes.
2. Stir in rutabagus greens and cook for 15 minutes. Stir in salt, sugar, hot pepper and lard.
3. Cover and cook on low for 1 ½ hours. Stirring constantly.

Boiled Okra Pods

Amounts	Ingredients
3 cups	water
1 teaspoon	salt
1 pound	okra pods
½	onion, minced

Directions

1. Add water and salt together and bring to a boil. Stir in okra pods.
2. Cover and cook for 15 minutes. Stir in onion and continue to cook for 10 minutes.

Smothered Wild Onions

Amounts	Ingredients
1 pound	wild onions, chopped
2 cups	water
2 teaspoons	salt
¼ cup	lard
6	eggs, beaten

Directions

1. Pick, clean, wash and chop wild onions. Place in a large black skillet and add Water. Boil for 10 minutes. Discard water. Add salt and lard and cook until tender.
2. Stir in beaten eggs and cook for 5 minutes.

Steamed Wild Asparagus

Amounts	Ingredients
1 pound	asparagus
2 cups	water
1 teaspoon	salt

Directions

1. Peel and wash asparagus. Boil in water and add salt.
2. Cover and steam for 10 minutes.

PRE-AND POST SLAVE REVIEWS

Africans, slaves and former slaves who were inventors (continued) in the United States

	Name	Inventions	Date Granted Patent
1.	Haines, J.L.	Portable Basin	Sept. 28, 1893
2.	Hammonds, J.F.	Apparatus for Holding Yarn Skein	Dec. 15, 1896
3.	Harding, F.H.	Extension Banquet Table	Nov. 22,1898
4.	Hawkins, J.	Gridiron	March 20, 1845
5.	Hawkins, R.	Harness Attachment	Oct.4, 1887
6.	Headen, M	Foot Power Hammer	Oct 15, 1886
7.	Hearners, R.	Seating Attachment	Feb. 15, 1878
8.	Hearners, R.	Detachable Car Fender	July 4, 1892
9.	Hilyer, A.F.	Water Evaporator Attachment for Hot Water Regulators	August 26, 1890
10.	Hilyer, A.F.	Register	August 14, 1890
11.	Holmes, E.H.	Gage	Nov.12, 1895
12.	Hunter, J.A.	Portable Weighing Scales	November 3, 1896
13.	Hyde, P.N.	Composition for Cleaning and Preserving Carpets	Nov. 6, 1888
14.	Jackson, B.F.	Heating Apparatus	Mar 1, 1898
15.	Jackson, B.F.	Matrix Drying Apparatus	March 10, 1898
16.	Jackson, B.F.	Gas Burner	April 4, 1897
17.	Jackson, H.A.	Kitchen Table	Oct. 6, 1896
18.	Lee, H.	Animal Trap	2/12/1867

19.	Lee, J.	Kneading Machine	8/17/1894
20.	Lee, J.	Bending Machine	6/4/1895
21.	Leslie, F.W.	Envelope Seal	Sept.21, 1897
22.	Leslie, A.L.	Window Cleaner	Sept. 27, 1892
23.	Lewis, E.R.	Spring Gun	May 3, 1887
24.	Linden, H.	Piano Truck	Sept. 8, 1891
25.	Little, E.	Bridle Bit	March 7, 1882
26.	Loudin, F.J.	Sash Fastners	March 21 1892
27.	Loudin,	KeyFastner	Jan.9, 1894
28.	Love, I.I.	Plastners Hawk	July 9, 1874
29.	Love, J.L.	Pencil Sharpner	Nov. 23, 1897
30.	Marshall, T.J.	Fire Extinguisher	May 26, 1872
31.	Marshall, W.	Grain Binder	May 11, 1886
32.	Martin, W.A.	Lock	July 23, 1883
33.	Martin, W.A.	Lock	Dec 30, 1890
34.	Matzelizer, J.E.	Nailing Machine	Feb. 25, 1876
35.	Matzelizer, J.E.	Machine for Distributing Tacks	Nov. 26, 1899
36.	Matzelizer, J.E.	Tack Separating Machine	March 25, 1890
37.	Matzelizer, J.E.	Lasting Making	Sept. 20, 1891
38.	McCoy, E.	Lubricating for Steams Engine	August 6, 1872
39.	McCoy, E.	Lubricator for Engines	Jan.20,1874
40.	McCoy, E.	Steam Lubricator	May 12, 187
41.	McCoy, E.	Ironing Table	May 12, 1874
42.	McCoy, E.	Steaming Cylinder Lubricators	Feb. 1, 1876
43.	McCoy, E.	Steam Cylinder Lubricator	July 4, 1876
44.	McCoy, E.	Lawn Sprinkler Devise	Sept. 26, 1899
45.	McCoy, E.	Steam Dome	June 16, 1885

46.	McCoy, E.	Lubricator Attachment	April 19, 1887
47.	McCoy, E.	Lubricator Attachment	September 29, 1891
48.	McCoy, E.	Lubricator for Safety Valves	March 24, 1887
49.	McCoy, E.	Drip Cup	Sept. 29, 1891
50.	McCoy, and Hodges	Lubricator	Dec. 24, 1889
51.	McCree, D.	Portable Fire Escape	Nov. 11, 1890
52.	Mendenhall, A.	Holder for Driving Reins	Nov. 28, 1899
53.	Miles, A	Elevator	Oct. 11, 1887
54.	Mitchell, C.L.	Phoneterium	Jan 1, 18844
55.	Mitchell, J.M.	Cheek Row Corn Planter	Jan10, 1900
56.	Moody, W.W.	Game Board Design	May 11, 1897
57.	Mooreland, R.	Reel Carrier	Oct. 6, 1896
58.	Murray, G. W.	Combined Furrow Opener and Stalk Knocker	April 10, 1898
59.	Murray, G.W.	Cultivator and Markers	June 5, 1894
60.	Murray, G.W.	Planter	June 5,1894
61.	Murray, G.W.	Fertilizer Distributor	June 5, 1894
62.	Murray, G.W.	Cotton Chopper	June 5, 1894
63.	Murray, G.W.	Planter	June 5, 1894
64.	Murray, G.W.	Combined Cotton Seed	June 5, 1894
65.	Murray, G.W.	Planter and Fertilizer Distribution Reaper	June 5, 1894
66.	Murray, W.	Attachment for Bicycles	Jan. 27, 1871
67.	Nance, L	Game Apparatus	Dec. 1, 1891
68.	Naster, H.H>	Life Pressing St.	Oct. 5, 1875
69.	Newman, Miss L.D.	Brush	Nov 15, 1898
70.	Newson, S.	Oil Heater or Cooker	March 22,1894

71.	Nichols And Latimer	Electric Lamp	Sept. 13, 1881
72.	Nickerson, W.J.	Mandolin and Guitar Attachment for Piano	June 27, 1899
73.	O'Conner and Turner	Alarm for Boilers	8/25/ 1896
74.	O'Conners And Turner	Steam Gage	8/25/1896
75.	O'Conners and Turner	for Alarm for Coast Containing Vessels	Feb 8, 1898
76.	Outlaw, J.W.	Horseshoe	Nov. 15, 1898
77.	Perryman, F.B.	Caterers Tray Table	Feb. 2, 1892
78.	Peterson, H.	Attachment for Lawn Mowers	April 30, 1889
79.	Phelps, W.H.	Apparatus for Washing Machine March	22, 1897
80.	Pickering, J.F.	Air Ship	Feb. 2, 1900
81.	Pickett, H.	Scaffold	June 30, 1874
82.	Pinn, T.B.	File Holder	August 17, 880
83.	Polk, A.W.	Bicycle Support	April 14, 1896
84.	Pugsley, A	Blind Stop	June 29, 1890
85.	Purdy and Peters	Design for Spoon	April 23, 1895
86.	Purdy and Sadgwar	Folding Chair	June 11, 1889
87.	Purdy, W.	Device for Sharpening Edged Tools	Oct. 27, 1896
88.	Purvis, W.B.	Bag Fastener	April 25, 1882
89.	Purvis, W.B.	Hand Stamp	Feb. 27, 1883
90.	Purvis, W.B.	Fountain Pen	Jan.7, 1890
91.	Purvis, W.B.	Electric Railway	May 1, 1894

92.	Purvis, W.B.	Magnetic Car Balancing Device	May 21, 1895
93.	Purvis, W.B.	Electric Railway Switch	Aug 17, 1897
94.	Queen, W.	Guard for Companion Ways and Hatches	August 18, 1891
95.	Ray, E.B.	Chair Supported, Device	Feb.21, 1891
96.	Ray, L.P.	Dust Pan	August 3, 1897
97.	Reed, J.W. Dough	Kneader and Roller	Sept. 23, 1884
98.	Reynolds, H.H.	Winder Ventilator for R.R. Cars	April 3, 1883
99.	Reynolds, H.H.	Safety Gate for Bridges	Oct 7, 1890
100.	Rhodes, J.B.	Water Clsoets	Dec. 1`9, 1899
101.	Richardson, A.C.	Home Fastener	Dec. 19, 1899
102.	Richardson, A.C.	Churn	Feb. 17, 1891
103.	Richardson, A.C.	Casket Lowering Devise	Nov.13, 1894
104.	Richardson, A.C.	Insect Destroyer	Feb. 28, 1899
105.	Richardson, A.C.	Bottle	Dec/12, 1897
106.	Richardson, W.H.	Cotton Chopping	June 1, 1886
107.	Richardson, W.H.	Child's Carriage	June 18, 1889
108.	Richey, C.V.	Car Coupling	June 25, 1897
109.	Richey, C.V.	Railroad Switch	Oct. 26, 1897
110.	Richey, C.V.	Railroad Switch	Aug. 3, 1897
111.	Richey, C.V.	Fire Escape Bracket	Dec. 28, 1897
112.	Richey, C.V.	Combined Hammock and Stretcher	Dec. 13, 1898
113.	Rickman, A.C.	Overshoe	Feb. 8, 1898
114.	Ricks, J	Horseshoe	March 30,1886
115.	Ricks, J.	Overshoes for Horses	June 6, 1899
116.	Robinson, E.R.	Electric Railway Trolley	Sept. 19. 1897

117.	Robinson, E.R.	Casting Composite	Nov. 23, 1897
118.	Robinson, J.H.	Life Saving Guards for Locomotive	
119.	Robinson, J.H.	Life Saving Guards for Street Cars	April 25, 1899
120.	Robinson, J.	Dinner Pail	Feb.1, 1887
121.	Romain, A	Passenger Register	April 23, 1888
122.	Ross, A.L.	Runner for Steps	August 4, 1898
123.	Ross, A.L.	Bag for Closure	June 7, 1898
124.	Ross, A.L.	Tensor Support	Nov. 28, 1893
125.	Ross, J.	Bailey Press	Sept. 5, 1893
126.	Roster, D.N.	Feather Curler	March 10, 1896
127.	Ruffin, S.	Vessels for Liquids and Manner of Sealing	Nov. 20, 1899
128.	Sampson, G.T.	Sled Propeller	Feb. 17, 1877
129.	Sampson, G.T.	Clothes Drier	June 7, 1872
130.	Scottron, S.R.	Adjustable Window Cornice	Feb. 17. 1880
131.	Scottron, S.R.	Pole Tip	Sept. 21, 1888
132.	Scottron, S.R.	Curtain Rod	August 30, 1892
133.	Scottron, S.R.	Supporting Bracket	Sept 12, 1873
134.	Shanks, S.C.	Sleeping Car Berth Register	July 21, 1897
135.	Shewcraft, Frank	Letter Box	
136.	Shorter, D.W.	Feed Rack	May 17, 1887
137.	Smith, J.W.	Improvement for Games	April 17, 1900
138.	Reynolds, R.R.	Non-Refillable Bottle	May 2, 1899
139.	Smith, J.W.	Lawn Sprinkler	May 4, 1877
140.	Smith, J.W.	Lawn Sprinkler	March 22, 1898

141.	Smith, P.D.	Potato Digger	Jan 21, 1891
142.	Smith, P.D.	Grain Bender	Feb. 23, 1892
143.	Snow and Johns	Liniment	Oct. 7, 1893
144.	Spears, H.	Portable Shield for Infantry	Dec 27, 1870
145.	Standard, J	Oil Stove	Oct. 29, 1887
146.	Standard, J.	Refrigerator	July 14, 1897
147.	Stewart and Johnson	Metal Bending Machine	Dec27. 1887
148.	Stewart, E.W.	Punching Machine	May 3, 1887
149.	Stewart, E.W.	Machine for forming Vehicle Seat Bars	3/22/1887
150.	Stewart, T.W.	Mop	June 13, 1893
151.	Stewart, T.W.	Station Indicator	June 30, 1893
152.	Sutton, E.H.	Cotton Cultivator	April 7, 1874
153.	Sweeting, J.H.	Device for Rolling Cigarettes	Nov. 30, 1897
154.	Sweeting, J.A.	Combined Knife and Scoop	June 7, 1898

MASSACHUSETTS TRAVEL REGIONS

9.Metro West

11. Johnny Appleseed Trail

BIBLICAL SCRIPTURES

PSALM 136:5

To him that by wisdom made the heavens: for his mercy endureth forever.

CHAPTER 33

BREADS AND BEVERAGES

Part I. Recipes That May Have Been Used by First African Slaves of Massachusetts for Breads and Beverages.

Corn Pones

Amounts	Ingredients
3 cups	corn meal
¼ cup	flour
1 teaspoon	salt
1 teaspoon	soda
2 tablespoons	sugar
1	Egg, beaten
1 cup	milk
¼ cup	lard, soften

Directions

1. In a bowl, stir together corn meal, flour, salt, soda, and sugar.
2. Stir together egg, milk and lard. Add to corn meal mixture.
3. Heat up corn pone pan and then add batter.
4. Cook over high heat until done.

Buttermilk Biscuits

Amounts	Ingredients
2 ½ cups	flour
1 teaspoon	salt
1 ½ teaspoons	soda
1 tablespoon	sugar
½ cup	lard
1 cup	buttermilk

Directions

1. Sift together flour, salt, soda and sugar in a bowl.
2. Stir in lard. Add buttermilk. Roll into a circle.
3. Make 8 biscuits. Bake in a pan.
4. Bake until golden brown.

Cornmeal Biscuits

Amounts	ingredients
2 cups	corn meal
1 ½ cups	flour
2 teaspoons	salt
1 ½ teaspoons	baking soda
2 tablespoons	sugar
¼ cup	lard
1 cup	milk

Directions

1. In a bowl, mix together corn meal, flour, salt, baking soda and sugar.
2. Cut into the lard and stir in milk.
3. Make into a ball and pat into a circle.
4. Make into 8 biscuits.

Gingerbread

Amounts	Ingredients
2 ½ cups	flour
1 teaspoon	salt
1 ½ teaspoons	soda
1 cup	lard
1 ½ cups	sugar
1	egg, beaten
1 cups	buttermilk
½ cup	molasses

Directions

1. Sift together flour, salt, and soda.
2. Beat together lard, sugar and eggs.
3. Add to flour mixture
4. Stir in buttermilk and molasses
5. To prepare a baking pan; grease and flour a pan and then add batter. Bake at a high heat.

Scones

Amounts	Ingredients
2 cups	flour
1 teaspoon	salt
1 ½ teaspoons	soda
2	eggs, beaten
½ cup	sugar
1 cup	milk

Directions

1. Mix together flour, salt, soda and beat.
2. Stir in remaining ingredients.
3. Drop on a pan and bake for 15 minutes.

BEVERAGES

Ginger Tea

Amounts	Ingredients
1 cup	ginger root, slices
1 gallon	water
1 cup	sugar

Directions

1. Prepare ginger root slices.
2. Boil in water for 10 minutes.
3. Remove slices and stir sugar in the hot tea.

Eggnog

Amount	Ingredients
1 quart	cream
6	eggs, whipped
1 vanilla	bean
4 cups	sugar

Directions

1. Mix together cream and eggs. Cook for 5 minutes.
2. Add in vanilla bean and sugar. Cook slowly and stirring vigorously until sugar is dissolved.

Wild Grape Wine

Amounts	Ingredients
10 pounds	wild grapes
3 gallons	water
5 pounds	sugar

Directions

1. Pick and wash grapes. Place in water and cook for 15 minutes.
2. Stir in sugar and cover. Drain after 5 days. Discard debris.
3. Cover and let stand for 6 weeks. Check weekly.

PRE AND POST SLAVERY REVIEWS

AFRICAN, SLAVES AND FORMER SLAVES INVENTORS (CONTINUED)

	Name	Invention	Date Patent Granted
1.	Taylor, B.H.	Rotary Engine	April 23, 1898
2.	Taylor, B.H.	Slide Valve	July 6, 1897
3.	Thomas, S.E.	Waste Trap	Oct. 16, 1883
4.	Thomas, S.E.	Waste Trap for Basins, Closets	Oct. 4, 1887
5.	Toliver, Georgr	Propeller for Vessels	April 20, 1891
6.	Tregoning and Latimer	Globe Supporter for Electric Lamps	3/21/1882
7.	Walker, Peter	Bait Holder	March 8, 1898
8.	Walker, J.N.	Shoemakers Cabinet or Bench	Feb. 3, 1890
9.	Washington, Wade	Corn Husking King Machine	8/14/1882

10.	Watkins, Isaac	Scrubbing Frame	Oct. 7, 1890
11.	Watts, J.R,	Bracket for Miner's Lamp	Ma7, 1893
12.	West, E.H.	Weather Shield	Sept.5, 1899
13.	West, J.W.	Wagon	Oct. 18, 1876
14.	White, D.L.	Extension Steps for Cars	Jan 12, 1847
15.	White, J. T.	Lawn Sprinkler	Dec.8, 1896
16.	Williams,	Camping Frame	2/2/ 1872
17.	Williams, J.P.	Pillow Stem Holder	OctobeR 16, 1899
18.	Winn, Frank	Action Engine	Dec. 4, 1888
19.	Winters, J. R.	Fire Escape LadddeR	MaY 7, 1878
20.	Winters, J.R.	FiRe Escape Ldder	April 8, 1877
21.	Woods, G.T.	Stea,	June 3, 1884
22.	Woods, G. T.	TelEphone Transmitters for	
23.	Woods, G.T.	Apparatus for Transmissions of Messages for Electricity	
24.	Woods, G.T.	Relay Instrument	June 7, 1887
25.	Woods, G.T.	Polarized Relay	July 5, 1887
26.	Woods, G.T.	Electro Mechanized Brake	Aug. 16, 1887
27.	Woods, G.T.	Telephone System and Apparatus	Oct. 11, 1887
28.	Woods, G. T.	Railway Telegraphy	Nov. 15, 1887
29.	Woods, G.T.	Induction Telegraph System	Nov. 29, 1887
30.	Woods, G.T.	Overhead Conducting System for Electric Railway	May 28, 1888
31.	Woods, G.T.	Galvanic Battery	August 14, 1888
32.	Woods, G.T.	Railway Telegraphy	August 28, 1888
33.	Woods, G.T.,	Automatic Safety Cut-out for Electric Circuits	Jan.1, 1889
34.	Wood, G.T.	Electric Railway System	Nov. 10, 1891

35.	Wood, G.T.	Electric Railway Supply System	Oct.31, 1893
36.	Woods, G.T.	System of Electrical Distribution	Oct. 13, 1896
37.	Woods, G.T.	Amusement Apparatus	Dec. 19, 1897
38.	Wormsly, James	Life Saving Apparatus	

MASSACHUSETTS TRAVEL REGIONS

11. Central Massachusetts

12. Greater Springfield

BIBLICAL SCRIPTURE

PSALM 141:1

Lord I cry unto thee make haste unto me: give ear unto my voice, when I cry unto thee.

CHAPTER 34

DESSERT COURSES

Part I. Recipes That May Have Been Used By the First African Slaves of Massachusetts for Desserts.

Sorghum Pie

Amounts	Ingredients
For crust	
2 cups	flour
1 teaspoon	salt
½ cup	butter
½ cup	cold water

Directions

1. In a bowl, stir together flour and salt. Cut in butter and add cold water.
2. Press out into pan for pie. Set aside

For Pie

Amounts	Ingredients
2 cups	sorghum molasses
1 cup	pecan halves
6	eggs, beaten
1 teaspoon	salt
½ cup	butter, soften

Directions

1. In a bowl, stir all ingredients together. Beat well.
2. Pour into pie crust.
3. Place pie pan into a larger pan. Bake until done and stiff in the middle.

Indian Pudding

Amounts	Ingredients
2 cups	milk
1	eggs, whipped
1 ½ cups	sugar
2 tablespoons	cornmeal
¼ cup	molasses

Directions

1. In a bowl, stir together milk, eggs and sugar.
2. Blend in corn meal and molasses.
3. Pour into a pan. Cover and bake over medium hot coals.

Raisin Pie

For Crusts:

Amounts	Ingredients
4 cups	flour
2 teaspoons	salt
1 cup	butter
1 cup	water, cold

Directions

1. Mix flour and salt.
2. Cut in butter.
3. Add water.
4. Divide into 2 balls.
5. Make into two crust one for top and one for bottom.

For Pie:

Amounts	Ingredients
2 cups	raisins
1 cup	water
2 cups	sugar
2	eggs, beaten

Directions

1. Place raisins in warm water for one hour.
2. Add sugar and cook until sugar is dissolved.
3. Cool and beaten in eggs.
4. Pour into top and bottom pie crusts and bake for one hour.

Coconut Cake

Amounts	Ingredients
3 cups	flour
1 teaspoon	salt
1 ½ teaspoons	baking soda
1	eggs, beaten
1 ½ cups	milk
2 cups	sugar
1 cup	butter, soften
2 cups	coconut, grated
1 cup	coconut milk
½ teaspoon	salt
½ cup	sugar
1 cup	cream

Directions

1. Prepare a large cake pan. Set aside.
2. In a bowl, stir together flour, salt and baking soda.
3. In a second bowl, stir together eggs and milk. Set aside.
4. Stir together sugar and butter.
5. Mix egg mixture with sugar and butter.
6. Stir in flour mixture and egg mixture; add 1 cup of coconut.
7. Pour into prepared pan. Bake 45 minutes.

Make topping:

1. Mix together 1 cup grated coconut, coconut milk, salt, sugar and cream in a pan and cook for 15 minutes. Cool and pour over hot cake.

Fried Peach Pies

Amounts	Ingredients
4 cups	peaches, cooked and mashed
1 cup	sugar
¼ cup	flour
½ cup	butter

Directions

1. In a pan, cook all ingredients together.
2. Cool and prepare crust.

For Dough

4 cups	flour
1 teaspoon	salt
1 cup	lard
1 cup	water

Directions

1. Combine flour and salt. Cut in lard.
2. Add water and make into a large ball.
3. Make into 8 balls. Roll out into 8 circles.
4. Fill each circle with filling. Seals sides and Fry.

For Frying:

1. Melt 4 cups lard in deep pan.

Persimmons Pudding

Amounts	Ingredients
2 cups	persimmons, mashed
1 cup	water
2 cups	sugar
½ cup	brown sugar
1 cup	milk
½ cup	butter

Directions

1. Boil persimmons in water until soft. Mash and add sugars.
2. Cook until sugars are dissolved. Stir in remaining ingredients.
3. Pour into a pan and bake for 30 minutes.

Mincemeat Pie

Amounts	Ingredients	
2	pie	crusts
3 cups	mincemeat, prepare	

Directions

1. Purchase mincemeat from the store and the Bake into double crust pie.
2. To make Double Crust: mix together 4 cups flour, 2 teaspoons salt, 2cups butter and 1 cup water. Stir together make into 2 balls.
3. Make Balls into 9-inch circles, to fit the size of pan.

Grits Pudding

Amounts	Ingredients
2 cups	grits, cooked
11/2 cups	sugar
¼ cup	brown sugar
1 cup	cream
¼ cup	butter, soften

Directions

1. Stir together all ingredients.
2. Bake for 45 minutes

Pre-and -Post Slavery Reviews

To help free the slaves, the 54th Regiment Massachusetts Volunteer Infantry- United States Colored Troops fought along with other colored troops in the Civil War. The Massachusetts Colored Troop

Trained near Boston and had many freed slaves as soldiers. The Massachusetts had more than 10 companies.

There were many colored troops that were captured or injured during the Civil War and they were imprisoned by the Confederate Troops.

54TH REGIMENT OF MASSACHUSETTS COLORED TROOPS PRISONERS

Taken from a list of AFRICAN-AMERICAN PRISONERS OF WAR AT CAMP SUMTER(ANDERSONVILLE PRISON)

Code number beginning with 1 or 2 soldiers buried in Andersonville National Cemetry3 soldiers

Reported to have died at Andersonville; 4 soldiers who have survived Andersonville and were able to Return home.

-54TH Negro Colored Troops who were prisoners of War at Andersonville, Georgia HA-Infantry

B -COMPANY

1. 44606 Solomon Anderson B-54
2. 44608 Daniel Bailey B
3. 44609 Jessie H. Brown
4. 44610 George Counsel
5. 44611 Alfred Green
6. 44612 Charles Hardy
7. 44626 William Henry Harrison
8. 44613 George Morris
9. 44614 William Rigby
10. 44615 Daniel States
11. 30456 William D. Vanalstylte
12. 44616 Charles Williams
13. 44633 James O. Williams

14. ---------Samuel B. Wilson

C

1. 13585 James Gooding -wrote letter to President Lincoln

D

1. 41359 Isaac Hawkins

F

1. 43253 William Mitchell
2. George W. Moshroe

G

1. 44624 Charles Stanton

MASSACHUSETTS TRAVEL REGIONS

13. Hampshire County

14. Franklin County

BIBLICAL SCRIPTURE

PSALAM 141:2

Let my prayer be set before thee as incense: and the lifting up of my hands as the evening sacrifice.

CHAPTER 35

SNACKS

Part I. Possible Recipes That May Have Been Used by First African Slaves of Massachusetts for Snacks.

Boiled Peanuts

Amounts	Ingredients
1 pound	green peanuts in shell of choice
1 gallon	water
1 cup	salt

Directions

1. In a large pot, stir together all ingredients and bring to a boil.
2. Cover and cook for 1 ½ hours.
3. Cool. Discard water. Serve peanuts.

Pickled Eggs

Amounts	Ingredients
1 dozen	hard- boiled eggs
1 gallon	distilled vinegar
¼ cup	salt

Directions

1. Boil and peel eggs. Place in a large jar.
2. Boil vinegar. Pour over eggs.
3. Let stand for one week.

Dried Peaches Slices

Amounts	Ingredients
12	peach halves, sun dried

Directions

1. Wash and dry peaches.
2. Remove pit do not peel. Place on cheese cloth.
3. Sun dry for one month.
4. Serve one peach half per person.

Hoop Cheese Slices

Amounts	Ingredients
1 pound homemade	hoop cheese

Ingredients

1. Slice hoop cheese into thin slices.
2. Serve 2 slices per person.

Fried Meat Skins

Amounts	Ingredients
1 pound	meat skins
1 pound	lard

Ingredients

1. Cut meat skins into 2 -inch squares.
2. Heat lard to hot. Fry skins.
3. Drain. Cool and serve.

Sugar Cane Joints

Amounts   Ingredients
1 stalk   sugar cane

Directions

1. Wash and disjoint cane.
2. Serve one joint per person.

Fried Peanuts

Amounts   Ingredients
1 pound   green shelled peanuts
2 cups   lard
1 tablespoon   salt
2 tablespoons   sugar

Directions

1. Shell and prepare peanuts.
2. In a black skillet, heat lard to hot.
3. Fry peanuts until golden brown.
4. Remove from pan and sprinkle with salt and sugar.

Green Apple Slices

Amounts   Ingredients
6   green apples, Sliced

Directions

1. Wash and core apples.
2. Slice apples and serve.

PRE AND POST SLAVERY REVIEWS

Continuation of Colored Prisoners at Andersonville, Georgia in the Civil War.

54th Negro Colored Troops

H Company

1. 44625 John N. Dickinson
2. 44628 Henry Kirk
3. 44629 John Leatherman
4. 44630 Joseph Proctor
5. 44631 Enos Smith
6. 44632 Frederick Wallace
7. 44633 James O. Williams

K Company

1. 43038 Jason Champlin
2. 43263 William H. Morris
3. 12304 William J. Smith

MASSACHUSETTS TRAVEL REGIONS

15. Bershires Region

16. Mahawk Trail Region

BIBLICAL SCRIPTURE

PSALM 146:1

Praise ye the Lord: Praise the Lord, O my soul.

REFERENCES

1. Holy Bible The Gideon International National Publishing Company, Nashville, Tennessee, 1978.

2. Federal Writers' Project: Slave Narratives Project, Vol.8, Maryland WPA-Slave Narratives: A Folk History of Slavery in the United States from Interviews with Former Slaves, Library of Congress Project Work. Property of Administration for the District of Columbia Sponsored by the Library of Congress -1936-1938.

3. National Park Service- List off Known African American Prisoners of War at Camp Sumter (Andersonville Prison) Andersonville, Georgia. 1863-1865.

NOW UNTO HIM THAT IS ABLE TO DO EXCEEDING ABUNDANTLY ABOVE ALL THAT WE ASK OR THINK, ACCORDING TO THE POWER THAT WORKETH IN US.

EPHESIANS 3:20

Printed in the United States
By Bookmasters